Think, Act, and Feel Better with CBT

PRACTICAL COGNITIVE BEHAVIORAL THERAPY TOOLS

FOR LIFE'S UPS AND DOWNS

Gianna LaLota, LMHC, LPC

ZEITGEIST • NEW YORK

To anyone struggling with their mental health—
may you find the strength to keep going

Zeitgeist™
An imprint and division of Penguin Random House LLC
1745 Broadway, New York, NY 10019
zeitgeistpublishing.com
penguinrandomhouse.com

ISBN: 9780593886014
Ebook ISBN: 9780593886007

Icons on pages 23, 45, and 55 © by Shutterstock/The Studio, on page 105 © by Shutterstock/pets scouts
Cover design by Michelle Black
Interior design by Emma Hall
Author photograph © by Erica Harris Devalve
Edited by Clara Song Lee

Printed in the United States of America
1st Printing

The authorized representative in the EU for product safety and compliance is Penguin Random House Ireland, Morrison Chambers, 32 Nassau Street, Dublin D02 YH68, Ireland. https://eu-contact.penguin.ie

CONTENTS

INTRODUCTION

As a CBT therapist, I've seen how cognitive behavioral therapy (CBT) can truly transform lives. It has helped my clients manage anxiety and depression, curb perfectionism and people-pleasing, and overcome procrastination, insomnia, and other challenges. I personally practice CBT techniques regularly to manage my stress and anxiety as well as address my own perfectionism and people-pleasing behaviors.

CBT is an evidence-based therapy that helps people understand the relationships between their thoughts, emotions, behaviors, and physical reactions so they can respond more skillfully to challenging situations. It teaches practical skills that anyone can use, even if they don't attend weekly therapy sessions. My clients often tell me how much they appreciate having so many CBT tools and techniques to implement in their daily lives.

Developing their CBT skills has helped my clients think in a more balanced way, regulate their emotions, overcome their anxiety triggers, and engage in behaviors that boost their mood and allow them to navigate life more effectively. This book can help you to do the same.

How to Use This Book

Think, Act, and Feel Better with CBT offers standalone guides for managing common, everyday mental health symptoms and conditions using CBT. Each guide offers insight on why the symptom or condition is so challenging, CBT tools and techniques to help you manage or overcome it, and exercises to practice and integrate into your daily life.

Start by reading chapter 1 for a brief history of CBT and to preview some foundational CBT principles that will come up in later chapters. Chapters 2 through 5 are collections of standalone guides that can be read in any order. I recommend starting with the condition or symptom that causes the most disruption in your daily life. Since many mental health conditions, such as anxiety and depression, occur at the same time, multiple sections may apply to you. In that case, start with the issue you wish to better manage first.

To get the most out of CBT, practice your new skills daily. Set aside a regular time each day to read one of the guides and do the exercises presented. Keep a pen and paper handy, or dedicate a notebook to this practice. Responding to the exercise prompts and taking notes will reinforce your learning. With consistent practice, you can seamlessly integrate CBT skills into your daily life to start thinking, acting, and feeling better.

CHAPTER ONE

How Cognitive Behavioral Therapy Works

Cognitive behavioral therapy (CBT) was pioneered by Dr. Aaron Beck in the 1960s and 1970s. While conducting research on patients with depression, Dr. Beck discovered that these individuals often had negative thoughts about themselves, the world, and the future. He introduced the term "automatic thoughts" to describe these recurring negative beliefs. Through his groundbreaking work, Dr. Beck developed the cognitive model central to CBT, which visually demonstrates how our automatic thoughts, emotions, behaviors, and physiological responses are interconnected (see figure 1.1). Since then, more than 2,000 studies have validated CBT's effectiveness in treating various mental health conditions.

The CBT Approach

Cognitive behavioral therapy, a powerful, evidence-based approach to treating mental health conditions and relationship problems, formed the foundation for the "third wave" of therapy, which includes approaches like dialectical behavior therapy (DBT) and acceptance and commitment therapy (ACT). Created by psychologist Marsha Linehan in the 1980s, DBT emphasizes mindfulness, emotion regulation, interpersonal effectiveness, and distress tolerance. ACT, which was developed around the same time by psychologist Steven Hayes, focuses on value-driven actions, acceptance, and mindfulness. In addition to using CBT, you'll practice techniques from DBT and ACT in this book, as these approaches are also valuable for mental well-being.

CBT is grounded in the fundamental principle that your thoughts directly influence the emotions you feel, the behaviors you engage in, and the way you feel physically in your body. These relationships are bidirectional—a critically important point to remember. This means that not only do your thoughts create your emotional responses, but your emotions can also influence your thoughts, and your behaviors can influence how you think or feel, too.

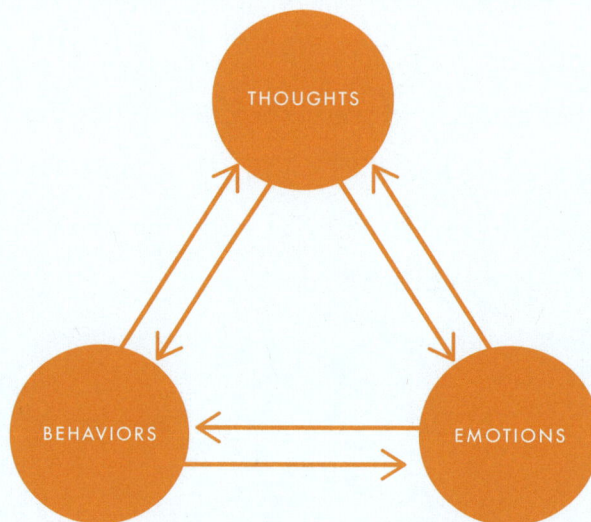

Figure 1.1: The Cognitive Triad Based on Beck's Cognitive Model

The cognitive model shows that it's not the situation itself that triggers your emotional response, but rather your thoughts about it. These thoughts shape how you interpret the situation and explains why two people in the exact same scenario can react with completely different emotions.

Consider this example: You're walking down the street, and you see someone you recognize. You smile and wave, but the person doesn't wave back. What goes through your mind in that moment? Do you think, "Oh no, they must have seen me and decided to ignore me"? Or do you think, "Maybe they were just lost in thought and didn't notice me waving"? Notice how each of these thoughts leads to completely different emotional responses. If you assume the first scenario, you might feel hurt, confused, or even angry. On the other hand, if you believe the second scenario, you might feel more neutral and understanding.

THE CBT PROCESS

Compared to traditional talk therapy, CBT offers a more structured approach, using various evidence-based tools and techniques. CBT is also goal oriented. In my work with clients, I help them set therapy goals to clarify their priorities for our sessions. These goals can range from "I want to communicate more effectively with my partner" or "I want to feel more confident in social situations" to "I want to learn to better regulate my emotions" or "I want to be less critical of myself." I then teach my clients CBT tools and techniques that help them achieve their goals. Outlining your goals helps you clarify what you want, provides a clear path forward, and allows you to track your progress. It's also motivating and empowering when you achieve your goals.

Take a moment now to outline a few goals for yourself on a sheet of paper or in your notebook. Ask yourself:

* What am I hoping to learn throughout the course of this book?
* What situations in my life would I like to manage more effectively?
* Is my mental health impairing my daily functioning in any way or holding me back from the life I want to live?

COMMON MYTHS

Let's debunk some common myths about CBT that I often encounter in my work. As you're doing this work, it's beneficial to release any expectations and assumptions you've heard rather than experienced.

Myth: CBT is meant to be only short-term and is completed within 12 to 20 sessions.

Fact: This myth likely stems from outcome studies that typically span 12 to 20 weeks. However, these studies don't fully capture the nuances of the therapeutic process. In practice, the number of CBT sessions required varies from person to person. For some issues, like treating a specific phobia, a shorter course of 8 to 10 sessions may be sufficient. However, those struggling with conditions such as depression or generalized anxiety can benefit from meaningful long-term support.

Myth: CBT does not address a person's past.

Fact: This myth likely arises because CBT often focuses on managing present issues before exploring the past. However, a skilled CBT therapist will explore a person's past to understand how their childhood and life experiences shape their current behavior and thoughts.

Understanding my clients' backgrounds, including their social and cultural upbringing, helps me gain a holistic view of them. First, I work with my clients to address automatic thoughts and then gradually uncover deeper layers, such as underlying rules, assumptions, and core beliefs formed in childhood. These core beliefs might include thoughts like "I'm a failure," "I'm unlovable," or "I'm not good enough"—which CBT can help change.

Myth: CBT is a rigid and cold approach.

Fact: CBT does incorporate structured exercises and techniques, but this is balanced with gentle activities that promote deep exploration, emotional processing, and validation. In therapy, there's often a warm and empathetic relationship between the therapist and client. So, in the way a therapist would, be patient with yourself throughout the process and show yourself compassion along the way.

CBT Skills

All the exercises in this book are drawn from CBT and CBT-related therapies. Let's take a look at the four categories of skills you'll encounter as you set out to do this work and what you can expect. You'll find clear, step-by-step instructions for practicing each skill in the standalone guides.

COGNITIVE SKILLS

Cognitive Distortions: Uncover the common unhelpful thinking patterns that can lead to difficult emotions. You'll learn to spot these patterns in your own thoughts and begin to challenge them. You'll find an overview of the most common cognitive distortions on page 17.

Thought Records: Use thought records to identify and challenge irrational thoughts. This tool combines several cognitive skills, like identifying "hot" thoughts (i.e., thoughts linked to strong emotions), gathering evidence for and against them, and developing more balanced thinking.

Underlying Assumptions: Dive deep into the core beliefs that shape your thoughts and behaviors and learn how to adjust them for a healthier, more flexible mindset.

EMOTIONAL SKILLS

Naming Emotions: Practice untangling or pinpointing feelings in the present moment. You'll learn to identify and name your emotions as they arise.

Self-Validation: Learn to validate your emotions and foster greater self-compassion. This is especially crucial if you were taught to question or suppress your emotions as a child.

Self-Compassion: Discover how to extend the same kindness to yourself that you readily offer to others. Cultivating self-compassion will help you navigate heavy emotions and develop a more encouraging inner dialogue.

BEHAVIORAL SKILLS

Behavioral Activation: Understand how your actions influence your mood. This skill helps you engage in activities that lift your spirits and enhance overall well-being.

Exposures: Follow practical, step-by-step exercises that help you confront and overcome your anxiety triggers, thereby reducing their power over you.

Graded Tasks: Tackle large projects by breaking them down into manageable chunks. Doing so can help you feel less overwhelmed, boost low motivation, and reduce procrastination.

Five-Minute Rule: Commit to spending five minutes on a task even when you don't feel like it. This technique is a game changer for beating procrastination and low motivation, especially if you struggle with depression or ADHD.

Sleep Hygiene: Cultivate healthy habits that promote better sleep quality. This is especially important if you struggle with insomnia or have sleep issues related to anxiety, depression, or other mental health conditions.

Habit Stacking: Seamlessly incorporate new, healthy habits into your life by pairing them with existing habits you already do consistently.

MINDFULNESS SKILLS

Mindfulness of Emotions: Approach your emotions with a sense of mindfulness and non-judgment. This will help you process heavy and more difficult emotions without judging yourself for feeling the way you do.

Mindfulness of Thoughts: Become aware of your automatic thoughts and your stream of consciousness. This practice helps you identify and challenge cognitive distortions in your thinking.

Mindfulness for Stress Management: Use various mindfulness techniques to activate your body's rest-and-digest response when your nervous system is triggered by stress and you need help feeling calm and relaxed again.

Grounding Techniques: Engage all your senses to connect to your body and be more present in the moment, especially if you spend a lot of time in your head due to anxiety or overthinking.

Thought Defusion Techniques: Learn to notice your thoughts as a mindful observer without judging them or assigning much weight to them. This technique from ACT has been proven to be much more effective than trying to suppress your thoughts and can be particularly effective for managing rumination, overthinking, and racing thoughts.

Common Cognitive Distortions

Don't believe everything you think. I remember the moment I realized that not all my thoughts were true. It was a major aha moment for me. Until then, I had never paused to question my automatic thoughts or understood how they influenced my feelings.

CBT helps us notice when inaccurate thoughts or thinking patterns negatively impact our emotions and actions. When our thoughts are based on faulty interpretations rather than on facts, they can lead to difficult emotions like sadness, anxiety, and shame. In CBT, we call these unhelpful thinking patterns cognitive distortions.

Cognitive distortions are normal and often develop from past experiences and learned behaviors. They can be influenced by our upbringing, past traumas, and even societal norms. Understanding their origins can help you be more compassionate with yourself as you learn to recognize, challenge, and change cognitive distortions.

To do this, you'll first need to learn to identify your automatic thoughts, which are the thoughts that make up your stream of consciousness at any given moment. Think of a situation that triggered a difficult emotion for you. Then ask yourself, "What was going through my mind right before I started feeling this way?" It may help to outline the situation, thoughts, emotions, and behaviors on paper.

Once you've identified your automatic thoughts, the next step is to label potential cognitive distortions in your thinking. Recognizing these distortions can help you understand why certain thoughts contribute to difficult emotions and allow you to challenge and reframe them more effectively.

The following are 15 common cognitive distortions with examples:

1. **All-or-nothing thinking:** Everything is either black or white. You think in absolute terms, failing to see the gray areas, or the nuances. For example, "I made a mistake, so I'm a total failure."

2. **Catastrophizing:** You make negative predictions about future situations, believing that things will be so bad you won't be able to cope. For example, "I'm going to fail my test, and it will ruin my grade for the entire semester."

3. **Labeling:** You put an unfair label on something, someone, or yourself. Labels are usually negative blanket statements. For example, "I'm such an idiot."

4. **Mind reading:** You assume you know what other people are thinking and feeling, believing you know their intentions without much evidence. For example, "Everyone at the party thought I was shy and awkward."

5. **Emotional reasoning:** You assume something is true because it feels true, and you use your emotions to guide your attitudes and judgments. For example, "Flying in planes is scary, so it must be dangerous."

6. **Selective abstraction:** You pay attention to only a few details, failing to see the whole picture. For example, "Even though my boss said I did a good job, I still think he's unhappy with my presentation because he corrected one of my PowerPoint slides."

7. **Magnification/minimization:** When evaluating situations, other people, or yourself, you magnify the negatives and minimize the positives. This can make a minor incident seem more important than it is. For example, "This disagreement with my friend means our friendship is doomed."

8. **Discounting the positives:** Positive points about yourself, a situation, or others are discounted or disqualified as if they don't count. For example, "They just invited me to be nice, not because they want me there."

9. **Overgeneralization:** Often using absolutes such as "always" or "never," you make broad overarching statements about the way things are. For example, "You're always in such a bad mood."

10. **Jumping to conclusions:** You draw conclusions with very little supporting evidence, taking an observation and running with it. For example, "My friend didn't text me back, so he must be upset with me."

11. **What-if:** You ask what-if questions about the future and what could potentially go wrong, focusing on what might happen in the worst-case scenario rather than on what is likely to happen. For example, "What if the plane crashes?"

12. **Unfair comparisons:** You compare yourself with others, believing they are better than you in some way, and make unfair assertions about your worth and value compared to them. For example, "My friends are all so much further ahead than I am in life."

13. **Blaming:** You unfairly place blame either on yourself or others depending on the situation. For example, "My sister started this entire fight."

14. **Personalization:** You assume other people's behaviors have something to do with you and take their actions personally. For example, "That cashier was so rude; I must have said something to upset them."

15. **Shoulds:** You use rigid "should" or "must" statements directed toward yourself or others. These "shoulds" reflect the way you wish things were rather than how they actually are. For example, "I should be better at this by now."

Practice Makes Progress

CBT emphasizes consistent practice of CBT skills for effective change. In my practice, I've noticed that the clients who make the most progress are those committed to practicing outside our sessions. For instance, my clients who struggle with social anxiety make the most progress when they regularly step out of their comfort zones and practice their exposure exercises, like speaking up in meetings or joining new activities to meet people with shared interests. Similarly, my clients who want to boost their confidence and self-esteem succeed when they commit to noticing their negative beliefs about themselves, use thought records to challenge those beliefs, and practice self-compassion regularly.

To create lasting change, you'll need to carve out time to practice the tools and techniques you learn from this book. Initially, it's beneficial to exercise your CBT skills daily. Establish a routine by setting aside a specific time each day to read and practice. Some skills can be practiced daily, while others can be used as needed.

TIPS FOR DAILY PRACTICE

Dedicate time. Set aside a specific time each day to read this book and do the exercises. Consider setting an alarm to remind you.

Keep a CBT notebook. Maintain a dedicated notebook or digital folder for your CBT exercises. If you choose to use sheets of paper, keep them together in a folder.

Track emotional triggers. Use your phone or your notebook to note moments when you feel emotionally triggered. This will help you identify patterns. You can also use thought records to explore and work through these moments.

Practice mindfulness. Pay close attention to the present moment in a nonjudgmental way. Use meditation, deep breathing exercises, or other activities to keep you in touch with your thoughts, feelings, and physical sensations.

Explore new skills. Practice different CBT skills, like exposure exercises, setting boundaries, and graded tasks, as situations arise.

Remember, be patient with yourself as you work through this book. Change doesn't happen all at once; it takes consistent effort and intention over time. The patterns you're aiming to change didn't develop overnight, so they won't disappear overnight, either. Often, these patterns have been reinforced for years. Give yourself grace as you challenge and change old beliefs and behaviors.

CHAPTER TWO

Manage Your Conditions

Anxiety

If you struggle with anxiety, you likely catastrophize and constantly jump to the worst-case scenario in your mind. This is your brain's way of trying to protect you from potential threats. However, thinking in this way likely just leads to increased anxiety in the long run. CBT for anxiety helps you to understand the way in which your brain works to protect you, identify unhelpful patterns in your thinking, and ultimately support you in challenging these thoughts.

There are different types of anxiety, including generalized anxiety, social anxiety, health anxiety, panic, and phobias. The common thread in all types of anxiety is the overestimation of threat combined with the underestimation of your ability to cope. This means that when you're anxious, your mind jumps to the worst-possible outcome and you believe it will be so catastrophic you won't be able to cope.

Symptoms of anxiety include:

* Feeling nervous
* Frequent worrying
* Restlessness
* Muscle tension
* Sweating
* Rapid heartbeat
* Difficulty concentrating

* Quick to startle
* Avoiding places or things that might trigger anxiety
* Frequent thoughts of danger
* Seeing yourself as unable to cope

THE CYCLE OF ANXIETY

Let's look at how the cycle of anxiety plays out:

1. You experience an anxiety trigger.

2. You practice avoidance, engage in a safety behavior, or seek reassurance.

3. You experience short-term relief.

4. Your anxiety persists in the long run.

This cycle is illustrated in figure 2.1.

Figure 2.1: The Cycle of Anxiety

Avoidance, safety behaviors, and reassurance-seeking can keep you stuck in the cycle of anxiety, because they prevent you from ever learning that you're capable of coping all on your own. Let's take a closer look at each:

Avoidance: Avoiding anxiety-provoking situations altogether. Examples include avoiding parties when you have social anxiety, avoiding planes when you have a fear of flying, avoiding spiders when you have arachnophobia, and avoiding exercise when you fear that an elevated heart rate will cause a panic attack.

Safety behaviors: Behaviors you engage in to make you less anxious when you can't engage in avoidance. Examples include going on your phone, sitting on the edge of the group, asking questions to avoid talking about yourself when you have social anxiety, and checking your heart rate when you have panic disorder.

Reassurance-seeking: Seeking reassurance that you are safe and that no bad outcomes will occur. Examples include asking friends if they're upset when you have generalized anxiety, looking up symptoms and scheduling additional doctor's visits to get second and third opinions even when you've been given a clean bill of health, and asking someone if they think you're going crazy when you have panic disorder.

CBT for anxiety helps you understand how your brain works to protect you. It guides you in identifying unhelpful thinking patterns and supports you in challenging these anxious thoughts. It also incorporates exposure therapy, which gently introduces you to your anxiety triggers and increases your exposure to them gradually, so you can build your confidence and enhance your ability to cope over time.

Thought Record

A CBT thought record is a valuable tool that helps you identify automatic thoughts, challenge unhelpful thinking patterns, and develop a more balanced perspective. Look at the blank thought record in figure 2.2 to familiarize yourself with the different prompts and the example in figure 2.3 to see how this might play out. You can record your answers in your notebook or on a separate page. Set aside 15 minutes for this exercise.

DIRECTIONS

1. Sticking to just the facts, describe a situation that triggered a difficult emotion for you.

2. List your thoughts, feelings, and behaviors with regard to that situation.

3. In the thoughts section, identify and label potential cognitive distortions in your thinking. For help, refer to the descriptions on pages 26–27.

4. For each thought, gather evidence that supports and/or refutes it. It's critical to stick to facts rather than your interpretations. When gathering evidence for each thought, consider:

    * Can I be completely certain this thought is true?

    * What's another way of looking at the situation I might not have considered?

    * If I shared this thought with a friend, what would they tell me?

5. Once you've gathered evidence on both sides, determine whether your initial thought is true or distorted. If the original thought is true, which it can be, then focus on problem-solving rather than on trying to change your thinking. However, if the original thought is a cognitive distortion, brainstorm a new, balanced thought. Ask yourself:

    * What new thought takes both sides of the evidence into account?

    * What's a more accurate way of viewing this situation?

6. Finally, say the new thoughts aloud and notice how you feel. Do you feel differently compared with how you felt at the start of this exercise? If so, you're experiencing firsthand how your thinking can shift the way you feel. How powerful!

SITUATION
What happened? Who? What? When? Where?

THOUGHTS
What was going through my mind? What was I thinking? What images did I have? What cognitive distortion might be present in my thinking?

EMOTIONS
What was I feeling?

BEHAVIORS
How did I respond behaviorally to the situation? What did I do?

SUPPORTIVE EVIDENCE
What evidence supports my original thought?

NON-SUPPORTIVE EVIDENCE
What evidence suggests that my original thought might not be true?

NEW THOUGHT
What is a more balanced thought that's based on the evidence?

Figure 2.2: Blank Thought Record

SITUATION

During a meeting at work, I asked a question about something that my boss had just explained. I was thinking about something else, so I missed my boss's original explanation.

THOUGHTS

My coworkers must be thinking about how that was such a stupid question.

Possible cognitive distortion: mind reading

EMOTIONS

Embarrassed
Anxious
Frustrated

BEHAVIORS

Kept my head down for the rest of the meeting and avoided eye contact. Left the meeting room quickly. Ruminated about the situation and replayed it over in my mind.

SUPPORTIVE EVIDENCE

• I asked about something that my boss had just explained.
• My coworkers were looking at me when I spoke.

NON-SUPPORTIVE EVIDENCE

• My coworkers are usually pretty nonjudgmental.
• They might not remember what happened.
• If someone else asked what I did, I wouldn't think anything of it.

NEW THOUGHT

My coworkers are likely not thinking about the mishap as much as I am since they're usually nonjudgmental. Not listening during that part of the meeting was an honest mistake and I'm sure other people have done it before, too.

Figure 2.3: Completed Thought Record Example

Exposure Hierarchy

An exposure hierarchy is a tool that's used to organize and plan for exposure exercises, which help you confront your anxiety triggers in a controlled and safe manner. This process is called desensitization. As you work your way up the exposure hierarchy from less anxiety-provoking situations to more challenging ones, you'll discover that your confidence increases, too. See the example on page 29 for some insight into how this might look for someone who has social anxiety.

DIRECTIONS

1. Brainstorm exposure ideas. Think about the situations your anxiety makes you avoid. What would you like to feel more comfortable with? What triggers do you want to overcome? Aim to come up with at least 8 to 10 exposure activities to try, including a mix of lower, mid, and higher levels of challenge.

2. Rate each exposure activity from 0 (not anxious at all) to 100 (the most anxious you can imagine). In CBT, this rating scale is called a Subjective Unit of Distress (SUD) rating.

3. Organize your hierarchy by arranging your exposure activities from most to least challenging based on your SUD rating.

4. Do the Exposure Activity on the next page. Start with the least challenging, and after you've made significant progress with that item, move up to the next level. This way, you can take small steps and gradually build your confidence.

EXPOSURE ACTIVITY	SUD
Give a presentation at work.	90
Ask someone out on a date.	80
Go to a group meetup.	70
Have a cup of coffee at a café alone.	60
Ask a question during a meeting.	50
Sit with my colleagues at lunch.	40
Make small talk with a cashier.	35
Say hi to my neighbors when I walk my dog.	30

Figure 2.4: Exposure Hierarchy for Social Anxiety Example

Exposure Exercise

Exposure exercises help you face your anxiety triggers head-on, empowering you to build confidence and resilience. If you haven't already completed the Exposure Hierarchy exercise on page 29, do so now. You'll need that information to move forward with this exercise. You can also review the example on page 31 before starting.

DIRECTIONS

1. Choose an exposure activity to complete, starting with the least challenging.

2. Prepare yourself for the exposure by noting:

   * What specific exposure activity am I practicing?

   * What are my predictions?

   * What safety behaviors will I refrain from during the activity?

   * What are my goals?

3. Do the exposure. Track your anxiety level on a scale of 0 to 100 throughout the activity. Notice the intensity of it and the rise, peak, and eventual fall.

4. Reflect on the exposure. After each activity, ask:

   * Did I reach my goals?

   * Did my predictions come true?

   * What did I learn? What are my takeaways from this exercise?

* Exposures are meant to be anxiety provoking. That's what makes them worth your time to practice.
* If your predictions about the exposure are rooted in anxiety, it's possible that the exposure exercise could go differently than expected. This is because anxiety overestimates the threat. What's more, negative predictions tend to be cognitive distortions, such as catastrophizing.
* Avoiding your safety behaviors is what makes an exposure a true exposure.
* Physiologically, anxiety will naturally subside on its own without you having to intervene at all. It will run its course.
* As you continue to practice exposures, you will notice two major shifts: (1) the intensity or peak of your anxiety will no longer be as high, and (2) the duration of time the anxiety lasts will shorten.

Here's an example of social anxiety exposure based on the exposure hierarchy on page 29.

Social Anxiety Exposure Activity Example

Before the exposure:

* What specific exposure am I practicing? *Sitting at a café and having a drink alone.*
* What are my predictions? *People are going to stare at me and judge me for being alone. The barista will be rude. I'll be so uncomfortable I won't be able to stand it.*
* What safety behaviors will I refrain from during my exposure? *Going on my phone, looking down and avoiding eye contact, sitting in the back corner of the café.*

* What are my goals? *Say hi to the barista, stay for 30 minutes, and avoid my safety behaviors.*

After the exposure:

* Did I reach my goals? *Yes, I avoided my safety behaviors, stayed for 30 minutes, and even said hi to the barista.*
* Did my predictions come true? *No, nobody stared at me. People were more focused on their own conversations and didn't seem to notice me.*
* What did I learn? What are my takeaways from this exercise? *My anxiety was highest in the beginning and then fell after about 10 minutes, my predictions didn't come true, and people were not as focused on me as I predicted.*

Additional CBT Tools

The following guides may also be helpful if you're struggling with anxiety:

* Chronic Stress (page 43)
* Fear (page 112)
* Inner Critic (page 62)
* Insomnia (page 151)
* Overthinking (page 84)
* People-Pleasing (page 159)
* Perfectionism (page 93)

In addition, these CBT skills may also be useful:

* Behavioral Activation (page 55)
* Best, Worst, Most Realistic Outcome (page 90)
* Designated Worry Time (page 87)
* Grounding Techniques (page 89)
* Locus of Control (page 113)
* Mindfulness of Emotions (page 129)
* Mindfulness of Thoughts Meditation (page 91)
* Practice Mindfulness and Body-Based Techniques (page 48)
* Thought Defusion Techniques (page 85)

Attention-Deficit/ Hyperactivity Disorder (ADHD)

Attention-deficit/hyperactivity disorder (ADHD) is a common mental health condition caused by neurological differences in the way the brain processes attention, motivation, and impulse control.

If you have ADHD, it can affect many areas of your life, such as academics, career, relationships, and daily activities. At work, sticking to deadlines and staying focused in meetings might be challenging. At home, you may find it hard to complete chores and stay organized. In your relationships, conflicts can arise if others feel they don't have your full attention or don't understand why you might be late or forgetful.

In my experience working with clients who have ADHD, I've also seen how it can impact self-esteem and self-worth, especially for those diagnosed later in life or without adequate support. Many people with ADHD blame themselves for difficulties in school or work, not realizing how much their condition contributes to these challenges.

These are the three types of ADHD and their common symptoms:

INATTENTIVE TYPE	HYPERACTIVE/ IMPULSIVE TYPE	COMBINED TYPE
Easily distracted	Unable to stay seated	A mix of both types with symptoms of each
Has trouble staying focused on tasks or activities	Difficulty waiting for one's turn	
Difficulty organizing tasks and work	Constant fidgeting, tapping, or squirming	
Forgets daily tasks and to-dos	Interrupts or speaks over others	
Often loses or misplaces things	Always revved up or on the go	
Struggles to effectively manage time		

If you don't have strategies and systems in place to manage your ADHD symptoms, daily life can feel overwhelming. Fortunately, CBT for ADHD can provide practical tools and techniques to help you stay organized, overcome procrastination, and accomplish your daily tasks successfully. It can also help you challenge any negative beliefs you may have developed about yourself due to ADHD, ultimately boosting your self-esteem and sense of self-worth.

Five-Minute Rule

ADHD brains can struggle with task initiation, especially when there's pressure, shame, or fear of failure. Relying on motivation alone isn't effective, as it tends to fluctuate. Instead, you need a strategy that helps you take action even when motivation is low. The Five-Minute Rule is designed to help you overcome the mental barrier of getting started. Once you begin and your brain is engaged, you build positive momentum. Even if you stop after five minutes, you've shown yourself you can start and make some progress toward your larger goals. And often, you'll find that once you start, you'll keep going.

DIRECTIONS

1. Set a timer for five minutes. This helps to create a clear, manageable time frame for your task.

2. Choose any task you need to accomplish, whether it's cleaning your bedroom, going for a run, starting an assignment, or paying a bill. Commit to working on it for just five minutes.

3. Once the timer goes off, take a moment to notice how you feel. See if the task seems less daunting now and if you're inclined to continue working on it. You can reset your timer for another five minutes if you'd like and see where that takes you.

Eisenhower Matrix

When there's a lot on your plate or your to-do list is a mile long, it can be challenging to know where to start or what to prioritize. As you contemplate all the things you need to do, you may feel paralyzed with indecision and overwhelm. Using the Eisenhower Matrix (which was developed by Dwight D. Eisenhower) can help you determine where to begin and where your time, energy, and focus are most needed. This framework organizes tasks based on their urgency and importance, allowing you to prioritize effectively.

DIRECTIONS

1. Draw the Eisenhower Matrix (see figure 2.5) on a sheet of paper or in your notebook. Leave enough space in each quadrant to write in your tasks.

2. With your to-do list in mind, determine which tasks belong in each of the four categories and write them in:

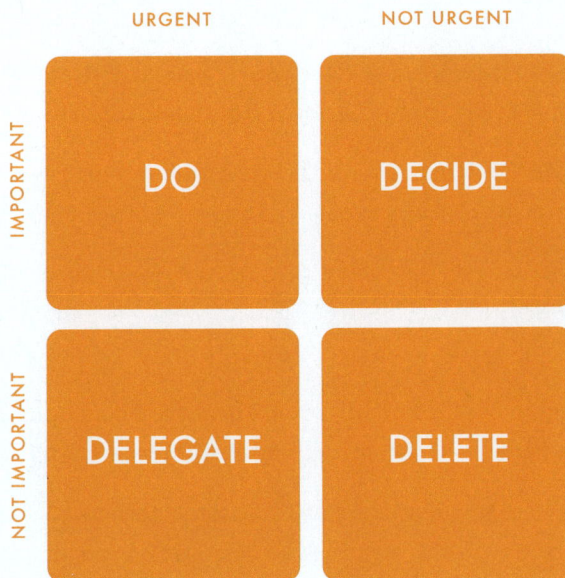

	URGENT	NOT URGENT
IMPORTANT	DO	DECIDE
NOT IMPORTANT	DELEGATE	DELETE

Figure 2.5: Eisenhower Matrix

Do: These tasks are both important and urgent. They have specific deadlines or consequences if not completed in a timely manner. This is where your focus and energy are required now. For example, submit a homework assignment, complete urgent client requests, and keep a scheduled appointment.

Decide: These tasks are important but not urgent. They have unclear deadlines but must be handled in the long run. For example, work on a long-term project, book travel for an upcoming trip, follow up with your friend, and go to regular self-care appointments.

Delegate: These tasks are urgent but not important. They don't require your specific skill set or expertise to complete. For example, researching your next vacation with friends, doing certain household chores, and planning the office potluck.

Delete: These tasks are neither urgent nor important. They are distractions and unnecessary. These tasks clutter your mind, so deleting them helps to free up mental energy to focus on other things. For example, sort junk mail, scroll through social media, and binge-watch the new series everyone is talking about.

3. Start working on tasks that are in the "Do" quadrant. Break them down into small, manageable pieces to make them more approachable.

4. For tasks in the "Decide" quadrant, schedule them in your calendar. Make a plan to return to them at a later date and take care of them, as necessary.

5. Recruit help for tasks in the "Delegate" quadrant. Find someone who can handle these tasks for you, freeing up your time for more important activities.

6. Eliminate tasks in the "Delete" quadrant. These are distractions that clutter your mind and prevent you from focusing on what truly matters.

7. Check and update your matrix weekly to ensure it reflects your current to-dos. This helps you stay organized and focused on your priorities.

Limit Distractions

Difficulty focusing is a major symptom of ADHD that can make it challenging to complete even seemingly simple tasks. Limiting distractions can help you focus more effectively by removing entertaining or tempting things in your environment that vie for your brain's attention. The lack of object permanence in ADHD means that when something is out of sight, it's out of mind. You can use this to your advantage by removing visual reminders of distraction.

1. Identify the task that needs to be handled.

2. Look around the area where you would normally do that task and try to identify what might distract you.

3. Eliminate the distractions before you begin the task. Here are a few ideas:

   * Put your phone on "do not disturb" or keep it in the other room while you're working.

   * Close any tabs on your computer that you're not currently using.

   * Keep your workspace clear to limit visual distractions.

   * Use apps that block your access to certain apps or websites at designated times.

CBT TOOL

Gamify Your Tasks

The ADHD brain craves newness, novelty, and stimulation. Gamifying tasks can help by stimulating your brain to release dopamine, which increases motivation and drive. There are many ways to add some playfulness to what needs to get done.

DIRECTIONS

1. Bring to mind a few tasks that you need to accomplish.

2. For each task, think of ways to incorporate game-playing elements into the process. Here are a few ideas:

    *   Break down larger projects into bite-sized chunks so you experience a sense of accomplishment more frequently.

    *   Reward yourself with something pleasurable after you accomplish a task to create a positive-reinforcement loop that encourages you to keep going.

    *   Compete against someone else to see who can finish a task faster. Adding a competitive element can make the task more exciting and engaging.

    *   Set a timer and challenge yourself to see how much you can get done in a set period of time, turning mundane tasks into fun races against the clock.

3. Approach one of the tasks with the mindset of a gamer who's ready to win the game.

CBT TOOL

Set Timers

Many people with ADHD struggle with time blindness—difficulty perceiving, managing, and estimating time. Instead of experiencing time as a smooth, measurable progression, the ADHD brain often sees time as "now" and "not now." This can make it challenging to accurately predict how long certain tasks will take, make it harder to keep track of time during the day, and cause you to get lost in tasks without realizing how much time has passed. Using timers throughout the day can help you manage your time more effectively.

DIRECTIONS

1. Familiarize yourself with the timer and alarm on whatever device you generally use.

2. Think about things you usually find it difficult to keep track of. For each of those things, set a reminder to prompt you to complete an activity and/or begin something else. Here are a few ideas:

   * Set daily alarms that go off at mealtimes so you don't skip meals.

   * Set a timer when doing your work for a designated period of time to stay on track.

   * Set an alarm to go off before you have to leave the house so you don't run late.

Additional CBT Tools

The following guides may also be helpful if you're struggling with ADHD:

* Inner Critic (page 62)
* Lack of Motivation (page 69)
* Low Confidence (page 77)
* Perfectionism (page 93)
* Procrastination (page 166)
* Shame (page 134)
* Unhealthy Habits (page 173)

In addition, these CBT skills may also be useful:

* Avoid All-or-Nothing Thinking (page 175)
* Cultivate Your "Why" (page 73)
* Graded Tasks (page 71)
* Identify Triggers and Cope Ahead (page 176)
* Improve Your Self-Talk (page 75)
* Pomodoro Timer (page 171)
* Practice Self-Compassion (page 67)
* Predict Time and Difficulty (page 167)
* Set Realistic Expectations (page 169)
* Start Small with Manageable Goals (page 177)
* Thought Record (page 25)
* Visualize How You'll Feel Afterward (page 74)

Chronic Stress

Stress is your body's natural response to fear, triggering hormones that prepare you to flee, fight, freeze, or fawn (pleasing or appeasing) in the face of danger.

For most people, stress is temporary. Once the stressor is gone, their bodies regulate and return to a calm state, switching from the fight-flight-freeze-or-fawn mode to the rest-and-digest mode. However, chronic stress is different. It occurs when the body remains in a heightened state of stress for prolonged periods of time, even without an obvious stressor. This can happen when ongoing stressors outweigh your ability to cope. As a result, you might feel perpetually stuck in fight-flight-freeze-or-fawn mode.

Stress manifests itself physically, emotionally, mentally, and behaviorally. Chronic stress, in particular, can make it harder to regulate emotions and may lead to mental health issues like anxiety, depression, and burnout.

In a state of chronic stress, you might:

THINK	FEEL	ACT
"This is too much for me to handle."	Worried about not getting things done	Procrastinate and put off important tasks
"There's no way I'm going to be able to do all of this."	Doubt in your abilities	Overwork yourself
"I don't have enough time, energy, or support to do all of this."	Overwhelmed by everything on your plate	Criticize yourself for not being able to get everything done
"This is impossible."	Muscle tension, headaches, difficulty sleeping, racing heart, sweating	Push through and try to do it all on your own
		Neglect healthy habits and regular self-care

It can be difficult to differentiate between stress and anxiety due to their similar physiological symptoms. Although they manifest similarly in the body, there are key distinctions between the two. Stress usually has an identifiable external trigger, such as a looming deadline or a challenging situation. It tends to go away once the trigger is resolved. Anxiety, on the other hand, can be more persistent and may not always have a clear external trigger. It can linger and affect your daily life even when there is no immediate cause.

When I work with individual clients who are under a great deal of stress, I always conduct a comprehensive lifestyle assessment regarding their sleep, diet, exercise, light exposure, and substance use. Taking good care of yourself when you're experiencing chronic stress can prevent it from getting worse. It's all about sticking to these basics:

* Get seven to nine hours of good-quality sleep each night.
* Eat regular nutritious meals throughout the day.
* Exercise regularly.
* Get sunlight exposure each morning.
* Limit your intake of alcohol and other substances that may disturb sleep.
* Create work-life boundaries.

* Develop a mindfulness practice.
* Make time to connect with friends and loved ones.
* Talk about your challenges with someone who can provide emotional support.

CBT encourages the use of healthy coping mechanisms, such as exercise, mindfulness, and relying on your social support network. It also helps you reframe your thoughts about your ability to manage daily stressors, boosting your confidence in your coping skills.

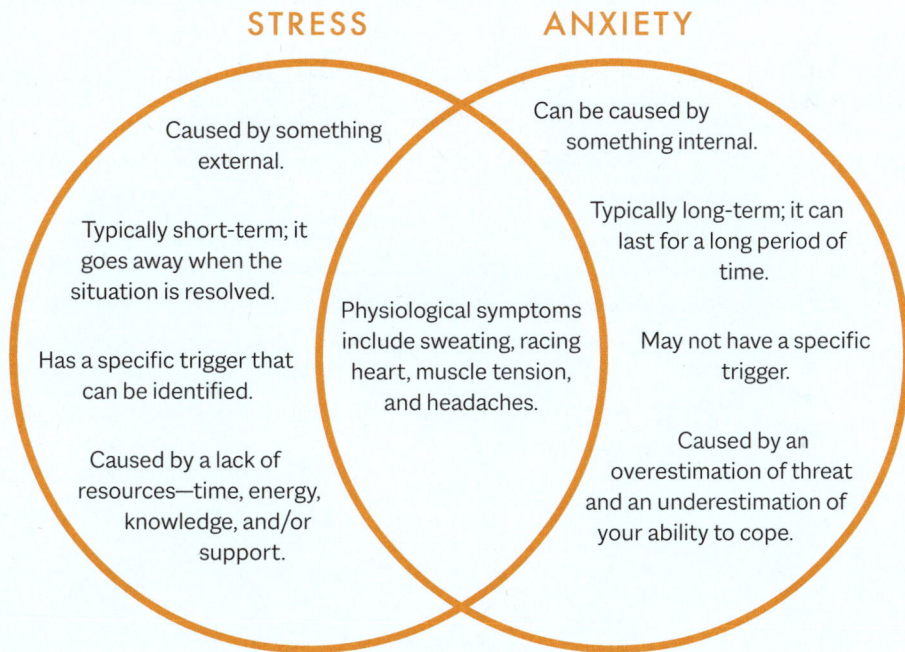

STRESS · ANXIETY

Caused by something external.

Typically short-term; it goes away when the situation is resolved.

Has a specific trigger that can be identified.

Caused by a lack of resources—time, energy, knowledge, and/or support.

Physiological symptoms include sweating, racing heart, muscle tension, and headaches.

Can be caused by something internal.

Typically long-term; it can last for a long period of time.

May not have a specific trigger.

Caused by an overestimation of threat and an underestimation of your ability to cope.

Figure 2.6: Stress and Anxiety Symptoms

Change How You Think About Stress

Notice where your mind goes when you feel stressed. What automatic thoughts arise? What do you tell yourself? Do you doubt your ability to handle your current stressors? One reason some people cope with stress more effectively is that they view stressors as challenges to overcome and believe in their ability to cope. Consider how these two very different responses to stress might sound:

UNHELPFUL RESPONSE TO STRESS	HEALTHY RESPONSE TO STRESS
"This is too much for me to handle."	"This is a really challenging time, but this season won't last forever."
"There's no way I'm going to be able to do all of this."	"I don't have to tackle this all at once."
"I don't have enough time, energy, or support to do all of this."	"I've coped with stressful experiences in the past, so I know I'm capable."
"This is impossible."	"This is an opportunity for me to develop my problem-solving skills."

DIRECTIONS

1. Grab a pen and paper or your notebook. Write down your automatic thoughts about your stress. What is the main thought or belief leading to your stress?

2. Write down how these thoughts make you feel and behave in response to stress.

3. Challenge your thoughts by asking yourself:

   * What stressors have I successfully coped with in the past?

   * Is it possible I'm more capable than I give myself credit for?

   * What strengths do I have that I'm ignoring?

   * Is there extra support I could be using?

4. Brainstorm new beliefs about stress that will better support you during this stressful time.

This exercise came in handy during my most recent move. Moving can be a massive stressor, especially in New York City. In the weeks leading up to my move, I noticed myself getting more irritable, feeling tension in my neck and shoulders, and doubting that everything would get done.

Once I became aware of these patterns, I paused and identified the main belief causing my stress: "There's no way all of this is going to get done." I reminded myself that this was my fourth move. Each time I've moved in the past, things have gotten done. That's a pretty good track record. Shifting my thinking to "Things always get done in the end" completely changed my emotional and physical state.

Practice Mindfulness and Body-Based Techniques

Stress manifests physically in the body, but practicing breathwork, mindfulness, and somatic (body-based) techniques can help you manage it effectively. These practices help shift your nervous system from a state of fight-flight-freeze-or-fawn to a state of relaxation.

The breath is a powerful tool because it is the only function of the nervous system we can directly control. We can use calming breathwork techniques to encourage our brains and bodies to relax. Try one or more of the following techniques to help you manage stress:

* **Body scan meditation:** Set aside 10 minutes. Get comfortable, either seated or lying down. Let your body be heavy. Close your eyes and deepen your breath. Elongate your inhales and exhales. Bring your attention to your feet. Notice any sensations or tension. Slowly guide your attention up your body, noticing sensations in your lower legs, knees, upper legs, pelvis, stomach, and back. Work your way up your arms, starting with your fingers, hands, forearms, biceps, and then triceps. Continue shifting your focus to your shoulders, neck, head, and face. Breathe as you do this. Notice the sensations without judgment.

* **Progressive muscle relaxation:** Set aside 10 minutes. Tense and then release isolated muscle groups, starting from your feet and working up to your head. Inhale as you tense each muscle group, and exhale as you release.

* **Diaphragmatic breathing:** Place your hands on your belly. Inhale, focusing on your diaphragm, rib cage, and stomach expanding. Exhale, allowing your belly to deflate. Continue for three to five minutes.

* **Box breathing:** Inhale through your nose for four seconds, hold for four seconds, exhale out of your nose for four seconds, and hold for four seconds. Repeat for three to five minutes.

* **Physiological sigh:** Take two sharp inhales through your nose followed by a long, extended exhale out of your mouth. This helps offload carbon dioxide and regulate your stress levels.

* **Mindfulness of emotions meditation:** Set aside 5 to 10 minutes. Get comfortable and deepen your breath. Place your hands over your heart. Notice how you're feeling at this moment. Notice how your emotions feel in your body. Name them. Say, "This is sadness," or "This is fear." Allow the emotions to be present without resisting them. Validate them and grant yourself permission to feel the way that you do without judgment. Continue to breathe as you feel the sensations in your body begin to shift.

* **Alternate nostril breathing:** Using your right hand, close your right nostril with your thumb and breathe in through your left nostril. Close your left nostril with your index finger and breathe out through your right nostril. Repeat on the other side and continue alternating for three to five minutes.

* **4-7-8 breathing:** Inhale through your nose for four seconds, hold your breath for seven seconds, and exhale out of your nose for eight seconds. Elongating your exhales helps signal your brain to relax. Repeat for three to five minutes.

* **Butterfly taps:** Cross your arms over your chest with your hands resting on your upper arms or shoulders. Alternate the tapping of your hands like the flapping wings of a butterfly. This uses bilateral stimulation to bring both hemispheres of the brain online so you can self-soothe. Continue until you begin to feel yourself relax.

Note: *I recommend practicing at least one of these techniques daily. Incorporate them into your morning routine to start your day on the right note or after work to create clearer work-life boundaries and transition smoothly into your evening. Regular practice increases your nervous system's capacity to tolerate stress and switch more easily between sympathetic and parasympathetic states.*

Additional CBT Tools

The following guides may also be helpful if you're struggling with chronic stress:

* Anxiety (page 22)
* Chronic Stress (page 43)
* Inner Critic (page 62)
* Overthinking (page 84)
* Perfectionism (page 93)

In addition, these CBT skills may also be useful:

* Best, Worst, Most Realistic Outcome (page 90)
* Designated Worry Time (page 87)
* Exposure Exercise (page 30)
* Exposure Hierarchy (page 28)
* Grounding Techniques (page 89)
* Mindfulness of Thoughts Meditation (page 91)
* Thought Defusion Techniques (page 85)
* Thought Record (page 25)

Depression

If you experience periods of sadness, low energy, and motivation, or struggle to feel pleasure and enjoy the things that you used to, then you may be experiencing symptoms of mild to moderate depression. While everyone occasionally feels low or sad, depression is more pervasive, affecting you mentally, emotionally, and behaviorally, with symptoms that can persist for weeks or months.

Symptoms of depression include:

* Sad or depressed mood
* Feelings of guilt or shame
* Less pleasure in usual activities
* More difficulty completing tasks
* Feeling hopeless about the future
* Isolating or withdrawing from others
* Feeling lethargic
* Difficulty focusing or making decisions
* Struggling with low self-worth
* Significant changes in weight or appetite
* Difficulty sleeping or sleeping more or less than usual
* Decreased sexual desire

As a therapist, I've noticed that people often have preconceived notions about what depression looks like. Many envision someone who cries often, feels intensely sad, or struggles to get out of bed. While this can be true for some, depression varies greatly from person to person and can range from mild to severe.

Depression impacts your thoughts, feelings, and behaviors. CBT addresses depressive symptoms at each of these levels:

THOUGHTS	FEELINGS	BEHAVIORS
Rumination over the past	Sadness, loneliness, or guilt	Isolation
Self-criticism for mistakes or perceived shortcomings	Hopelessness about the future	Reduced activity
Pessimism about improvement	Lethargy or low motivation	Loss of interest in enjoyable activities
Suicidal thoughts or thoughts of death	Emptiness or numbness	Irregular eating or sleeping patterns
	Shame for experiencing depression	Difficulty completing work or school tasks

Like all mental health conditions, depression results from a combination of biological, psychological, and social factors. Adverse life events, such as stressful transitions, trauma, grief, unemployment, poverty, and social isolation, can increase the likelihood of depression. A family history of depression or other mood disorders can also predispose someone to experience depression.

Depression can zap your energy and motivation, making it harder to accomplish daily tasks, stay active, and connect with others. Inactivity and isolation can worsen your mood, creating a vicious cycle.

CBT for depression uses a technique known as behavioral activation to help you understand the connection between your behaviors and your mood and to take action by engaging in activities that can enhance your mood. CBT also helps you challenge common depressive thinking patterns, such as all-or-nothing thinking, selective abstraction, and unfair comparisons. Developing more balanced ways of thinking can help you perceive yourself, others, challenging situations, and the future more accurately.

Wheel of Life

The Wheel of Life tool helps you assess your level of satisfaction in various areas of your life. By rating each area, you can identify minor changes to increase your overall satisfaction. This assessment is particularly helpful for people who are focused on overcoming their depression, as it allows them to track their progress and measure their improvements over time.

DIRECTIONS

1.   Draw the Wheel of Life (below) on a piece of paper or in your notebook.

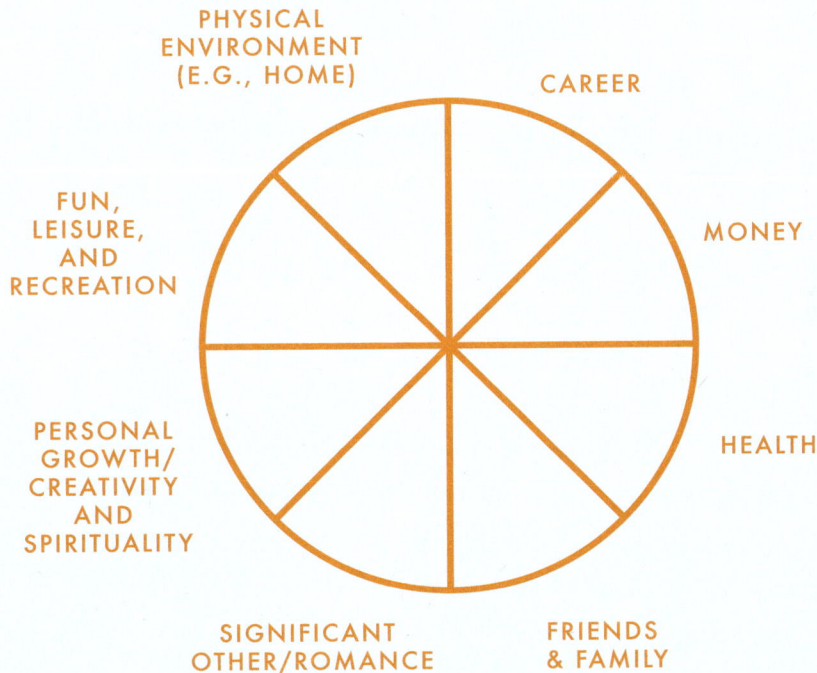

Figure 2.7: Wheel of Life Pie Chart, adapted from Paul J. Meyer's Wheel of Life tool

2. On a scale from 1 (completely dissatisfied) to 10 (very satisfied), rate your level of satisfaction in each area.

3. Review your ratings and notice any patterns. Are your scores as expected, or do they surprise you? How do they relate to the depression you've been experiencing?

4. Set small goals to bump up your ratings. Identify areas to prioritize first. Where can you achieve small wins? What minor changes could boost your scores in various areas? For example, if you rated your satisfaction with friends at a 4, you could set an intention to call a friend weekly or join a book club to meet new people, bumping this score up to a 5 or above.

5. Save your initial ratings for future reference. After working toward your small goals, revisit this exercise in a month and re-rate your satisfaction. Consider making this a monthly ritual to track your progress over time.

Behavioral Activation

When struggling with depression, it can be challenging to engage in regular activities and feel the same level of pleasure or accomplishment as before. Depression can drain your energy, motivation, and feelings of pleasure, making it difficult to do anything at all. This often leads to a cycle of retreating, isolating, and remaining inactive, which perpetuates the depressed state.

Behavioral activation aims to break this cycle by encouraging you to get active with the intention of supporting your mood. Specifically, you can intentionally plan activities that provide pleasure, accomplishment, and connection.

* **Pleasure:** Doing activities you enjoy helps you experience happiness and live more fully.
* **Accomplishment:** Challenging yourself allows for growth and development, giving you a sense of achievement.
* **Connection:** Building relationships with others makes you feel valued and connected.

The more you engage in these behaviors, the better you will feel; this is illustrated in figure 2.8.

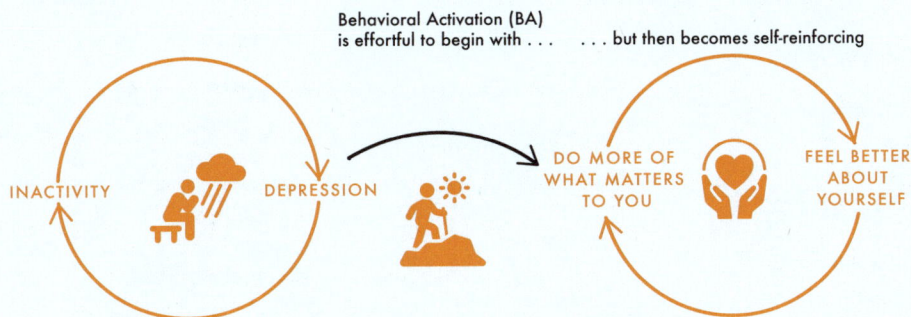

Behavioral Activation (BA)
is effortful to begin with . . .   . . . but then becomes self-reinforcing

INACTIVITY — DEPRESSION — DO MORE OF WHAT MATTERS TO YOU — FEEL BETTER ABOUT YOURSELF

Figure 2.8: Behavioral Activation in Action

1. Track your mood on your phone or in your notebook for the next seven days at two or three set intervals throughout the day. Note the corresponding activity you're doing when you feel a particular way. Set an alarm on your phone to go off at these set intervals to remind you to track. This ensures accurate ratings, as it is easy to forget exactly how you were feeling in the moment if you wait too long.

2. Notice patterns. Reflect on your mood and activities over the week. What were you doing when you felt your best? What about when you felt your worst? Identify moments when you felt pleasure, accomplishment, and connection. Was there a relationship between your mood and your level of activity?

3. Plan activities. Using the insights from tracking your mood, plan your week to include activities that provide pleasure, accomplishment, and connection.

4. Create an activities menu with a list of options to choose from. Notice how you feel before and after engaging in these activities. Here are some ideas:

TO HELP YOU FEEL PLEASURE	TO HELP YOU FEEL ACCOMPLISHED	TO HELP YOU FEEL CONNECTED
Watch a funny show.	Work out.	Call a family member.
Eat at a new restaurant.	Clean your bedroom.	Meet a friend for coffee.
Listen to upbeat music.	Do household chores.	Say hi to your neighbors or coworkers.
Spend time outside.	Do a small task that you've been putting off.	Join a book club.
Read a book for fun.	Cook yourself a meal.	Volunteer for a cause you care about.
Try something new.	Accomplish something off your to-do list.	Do a random small act of kindness.
Paint, draw, or do something creative.	Learn a new skill.	Send a message to an old friend.
Explore your neighborhood.	Complete a work project or school assignment.	
Play with your pet.		

Tips to keep in mind to get the most out of behavioral activation:

* **Start with small, achievable goals.** If going to a workout class feels too daunting, commit to going for a 10-minute walk around the neighborhood. You want to set yourself up for success, not failure. You can increase your goals over time as you create positive momentum.
* **Don't expect to feel better right away.** It will likely take time before you begin to feel pleasure or a sense of accomplishment again. This is a normal part of the process.
* **Celebrate your wins.** Sometimes even doing daily tasks like taking a shower or making yourself a meal can feel insurmountable when you're experiencing depression. Give yourself credit for everything that you do no matter how small or big it may seem.

IMPORTANT NOTE: *If you are experiencing persistent depression, seek out the help of a mental health provider. If you are struggling with thoughts of suicide, call the Suicide & Crisis Lifeline at 988.*

Additional CBT Tools

The following guides may also be helpful if you're struggling with depression:

* Guilt (page 118)
* Inner Critic (page 62)
* Insomnia (page 151)
* Lack of Motivation (page 69)
* Low Confidence (page 77)
* Sadness (page 125)
* Shame (page 134)

In addition, these CBT skills may also be useful:

* Avoid All-or-Nothing Thinking (page 175)
* Build Mastery (page 82)
* Challenge Your "Positive" Beliefs About Self-Criticism (page 65)
* Combat Comparison (page 79)
* Create a Credits List (page 81)
* Do a Strengths Inventory (page 80)
* Get to Know Your Inner Critic (page 64)
* Identify Triggers and Cope Ahead (page 176)
* Mindfulness of Emotions (page 129)
* Practice Self-Acceptance and Self-Compassion (page 139)
* Practice Self-Compassion (page 67)
* Practice Self-Forgiveness (page 123)
* Share in Safe Spaces (page 140)
* Start Small with Manageable Goals (page 177)
* Thought Record (page 25)
* Uncover Negative Core Beliefs (page 136)
* Validate Your Feelings (page 127)

CHAPTER THREE

Challenge Your Thought Patterns

Inner Critic

If you often find yourself pointing out your own faults or speaking harshly to yourself, you might have a problem with self-criticism. This is often referred to as the inner critic in popular psychology. Think of the inner critic as the voice in your head that judges and criticizes you. Sometimes, this voice can sound like a parent or caregiver from your childhood who was critical of you. Other times, it might come from a perfectionist part of you that never feels adequate. By identifying this voice as the inner critic, you can start to see it as separate from your true self.

Here are some signs that you struggle with self-criticism:

* Constantly criticizing yourself and feeling bad about what you did or said
* Having a negative internal dialogue and speaking harshly to yourself
* Quickly pointing out your faults while ignoring your strengths
* Ruminating over past actions or words
* Finding it hard to forgive yourself or show compassion to yourself
* Struggling with low self-esteem and a negative self-image

There are several reasons you might be more critical of yourself than others. Early childhood experiences play a significant role, especially if you received frequent criticism from caregivers. Maybe your caregivers were quick to punish you for a bad grade or harshly judged your athletic performance. You might have also seen a caregiver being critical of themselves, modeling this behavior for you. Intense self-criticism is often linked to trauma and abuse, especially if these experiences have shaped negative core beliefs about yourself and your self-worth.

Self-criticism can seriously harm your mental health. It damages your self-esteem, making you focus on perceived shortcomings and ignore your strengths. Self-criticism is also strongly correlated with mental health conditions such as depression, anxiety, and perfectionism. Having a strong inner critic creates a vicious cycle in which you never feel good enough.

Popular psychology often villainizes the inner critic and encourages you to banish it. This approach is ineffective and overlooks how the inner critic is actually trying to help you. Deep down, the inner critic is a part of you, and it wants to protect you by motivating you. For example, it might push you toward perfection to avoid failure and disappointment. Understanding these intentions can help you work with your inner critic rather than against it. CBT can help you understand the function of your inner critic and the purpose it serves, including its protective role. CBT also helps you challenge your subconscious "positive" beliefs about self-criticism and work toward cultivating greater self-compassion, which is the antidote to self-criticism.

Get to Know Your Inner Critic

Understanding your inner critic is crucial because it helps you recognize the root of negative self-talk, allowing you to challenge and reframe these harmful beliefs and ultimately foster self-compassion. Knowing what triggers it, what it says, and how it tries to protect you will enable you to work with it mindfully. We often try to push our inner critic to the side or suppress it to combat it. However, it's all about taking a gentler approach to the inner critic within and to yourself as a whole.

DIRECTIONS

1. Go somewhere you will not be disturbed for at least 15 minutes.

2. In your notebook or on a sheet of paper, journal your answers to the following prompts:

    *   How aware am I of my inner critic?

    *   What types of situations trigger my inner critic?

    *   What does my inner critic say to me and how does it speak to me?

    *   What purpose does my inner critic serve?

    *   What is my inner critic trying to protect me from or prevent from happening?

    *   What am I afraid would happen if I am compassionate toward myself instead of critical?

    *   What prevents me from showing myself compassion?

    *   How would I feel if I showed myself compassion instead of criticizing myself?

3. Use the insight from your answers to start practicing self-compassion.

Challenge Your "Faulty" Beliefs About Self-Criticism

When working with clients who struggle with intense self-criticism, I often find they are resistant to letting go of it entirely. Why? Because they hold subconscious beliefs about how their inner critic helps them. On some level, they believe their inner critic motivates them, gives them an edge, or drives their success. Challenging these beliefs is a crucial step toward letting go of self-criticism and cultivating self-compassion, which is a far greater motivator. Some common faulty beliefs about self-criticism include:

* "Self-criticism helps motivate me."
* "I have to be hard on myself to achieve my goals."
* "Being compassionate instead of critical will make me lose my edge."
* "If I'm not hard on myself, I won't be successful."
* "If I don't constantly push myself, I'll be lazy and complacent."

DIRECTIONS

1. What are some of your beliefs about self-criticism. Do you think it's necessary to be critical of yourself? Do you believe it serves or motivates you? Find out by conducting an experiment.

2. On day 1, criticize yourself every time you make a mistake, struggle with low motivation, or attempt to take action. Notice how that feels and the behaviors that follow.

3. On day 2, speak to yourself with compassion and kindness in these same types of moments. Notice how that feels and the behaviors that follow.

4. On day 3, reflect on what you learned from this exercise. Was it criticism or compassion that served as a healthier and more productive motivator?

5. Write out the new beliefs you want to develop about self-compassion. Here are a few ideas:

   * "Self-compassion is a better motivator than self-criticism."

   * "I am not successful because of my inner critic but despite it."

   * "I choose to approach my goals from a place of compassion, not criticism."

   * "I respond far better to compassion than to criticism."

Practice Self-Compassion

Self-compassion involves treating yourself with care, concern, and sensitivity. One powerful way to cultivate self-compassion is to speak to yourself the way you would speak to a friend. This is especially effective if you find it easier to extend compassion to others than to yourself. Another way is to journal without judgment. Write about your feelings, especially in moments of suffering, to cultivate a deeper sense of self-compassion. Yet another way is to notice what self-compassion feels like in your physical body; that's the goal of this exercise.

DIRECTIONS

1. Find a comfortable position, either seated or lying down. Close your eyes.

2. Bring one hand to your heart and one to your belly. Feel the connection and warmth from your hands. Deepen your breath, elongating your inhales and exhales.

3. Bring to mind a situation in which you were moderately critical of yourself. Visualize yourself in that scene. Notice any emotions or physical sensations that arise. Breathe through them.

4. Ask your inner critic to step aside so you can invite in a sense of compassion. Take your hands and rub your palms together to create heat, then place them over your heart. Imagine sending warmth, light, and compassion to the version of yourself in the previous scene.

5. Tell yourself what you needed to hear at that time, such as, "Everybody makes mistakes," "You did the best you could," or "I can see that this is a difficult time for you." Continue to breathe as you do this. Notice how this feels in your physical body.

6. Let the image of that scene fade. Return your focus to the here and now. Take one final deep breath in and out before opening your eyes. Allow yourself to bask in the feeling of compassion.

Additional CBT Tools

The following guides may also be helpful if you're struggling with self-criticism:

* Depression (page 51)
* Guilt (page 118)
* Lack of Motivation (page 69)
* Low Confidence (page 77)
* Perfectionism (page 93)
* Sadness (page 125)
* Shame (page 134)

In addition, these CBT skills may also be useful:

* Avoid All-or-Nothing Thinking (page 175)
* Challenge Rules and Assumptions (page 97)
* Do a Strengths Inventory (page 80)
* Mindfulness of Thoughts Meditation (page 91)
* Practice Self-Acceptance and Self-Compassion (page 139)
* Thought Record (page 25)
* Behavioral Experiment (page 99)
* Uncover Negative Core Beliefs (page 136)

Lack of Motivation

Motivation is the driving force behind our actions, enabling us to achieve our goals. It can be extrinsic, driven by external factors like rewards or approval, or intrinsic, coming from within and often more sustainable in the long term. Examples of extrinsic motivation include earning a higher salary, receiving a good grade, or gaining approval from others. Intrinsic motivation, on the other hand, might involve running for the sheer joy of it or learning something new out of pure interest.

Feeling a lack of motivation can be frustrating and hinder your ability to accomplish both small and large goals. While motivation naturally ebbs and flows, consistent low motivation can be a sign of an underlying issue such as depression or ADHD, which can negatively impact your sense of determination or enthusiasm.

Several common myths about motivation can keep you feeling stuck. One of the biggest misconceptions is that motivation must come before action. In reality, it's the opposite. Taking action can actually generate motivation.

Believing that motivation must come first might lead you to wait around for a spark that never arrives. Understanding that action precedes motivation can empower you to take small steps. If you've ever struggled to start something but found that, once you began, you got into a groove, then you've experienced firsthand how motivation follows action.

Here are the most common myths about motivation and some truths to help remind yourself as you go about your week:

MYTHS ABOUT MOTIVATION	TRUTHS ABOUT MOTIVATION
Motivation must come before taking action.	You cultivate motivation through action.
You need to feel motivated to do something.	You can do something even when you don't feel like it.
You're either a motivated person or you're not.	Motivation is not an inherent trait a person possesses.
Motivation is the most important ingredient of your success.	Many factors contribute to someone's success.
Motivation should remain consistent over time.	Motivation naturally ebbs and flows.

CBT helps you understand that action precedes motivation and provides you with a number of effective strategies that make it easier to take action, cultivating sustainable motivation that drives you in the long term. When you clearly define your values and set goals that align with them, you create a strong sense of purpose—a "why"—that can drive you to take actions that are in line with those values.

Graded Tasks

Graded tasks help you break larger projects down into smaller steps so that you clearly understand how to start and where your effort and energy is needed. Graded tasks also help combat overwhelm by focusing on one small step rather than on the entire staircase. You can use a graded task for big or small projects. For example, if your goal is to go for a run, start by picking out an outfit and getting dressed. By breaking the goal down bit by bit, you'll find yourself out the door and running before you know it. Here are two examples to see how this exercise plays out.

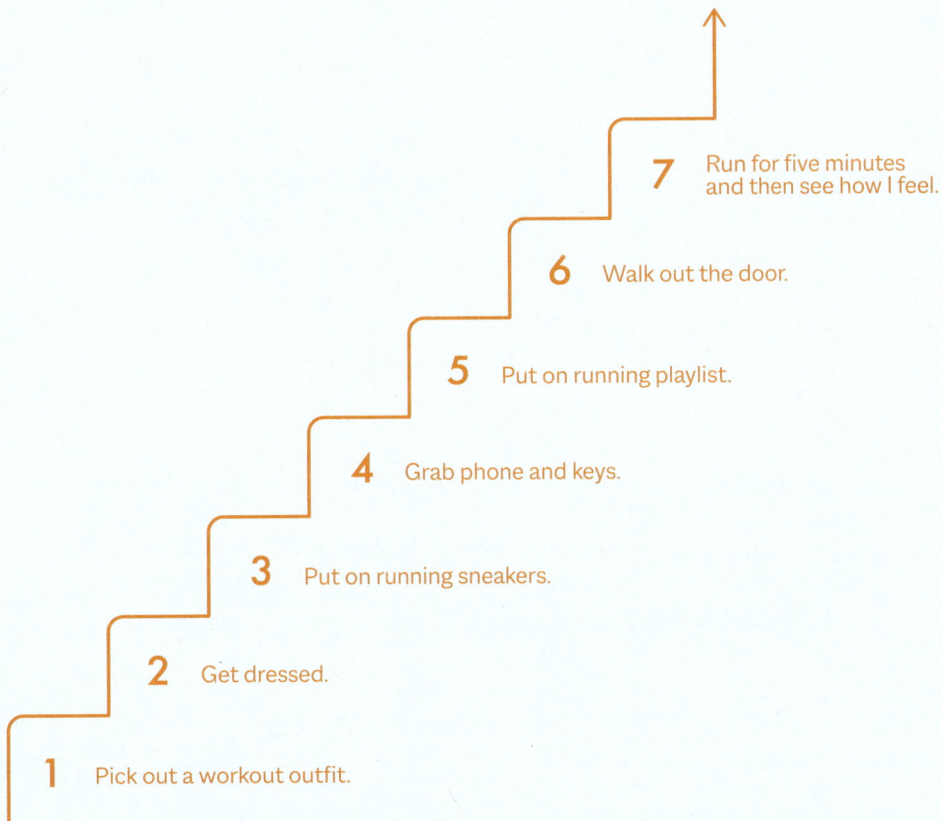

7 Run for five minutes and then see how I feel.

6 Walk out the door.

5 Put on running playlist.

4 Grab phone and keys.

3 Put on running sneakers.

2 Get dressed.

1 Pick out a workout outfit.

Figure 3.1: Example of a Graded Task for Going for a Run

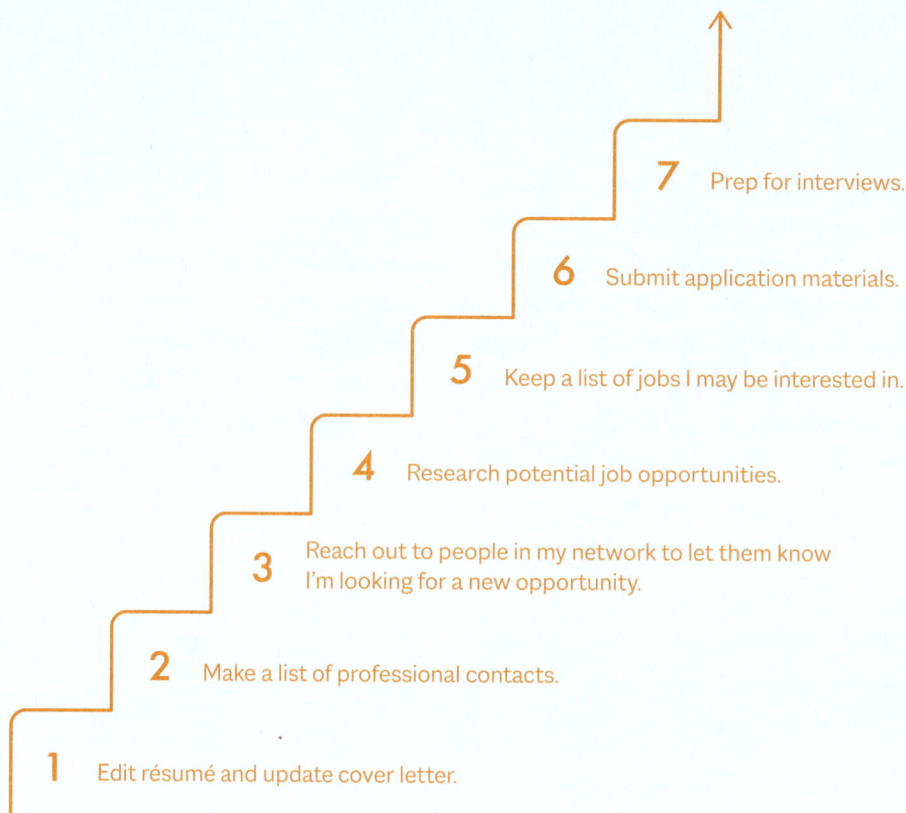

7 Prep for interviews.

6 Submit application materials.

5 Keep a list of jobs I may be interested in.

4 Research potential job opportunities.

3 Reach out to people in my network to let them know I'm looking for a new opportunity.

2 Make a list of professional contacts.

1 Edit résumé and update cover letter.

Figure 3.2: Example of a Graded Task for Finding a New Job

DIRECTIONS

1. On a piece of paper or in your notebook, draw the outline of steps as shown in the examples.

2. Pick any task that feels daunting that you'd like to tackle. Break it down into small, actionable steps. Make each individual step as manageable as possible.

3. Label each step from bottom to top with the incremental action steps you've outlined.

4. Focus on the first step and resist the urge to jump ahead or worry about future steps until you reach them.

Cultivate Your "Why"

It's natural for motivation to ebb and flow. In moments of low motivation, reflecting on your "why" can help. Let's say my client's goal is to work out three times per week. As a young parent, she knows the importance of taking care of her health, especially with a family history of diabetes. Despite this, she finds it challenging to stick to her goal. My advice to her is to reflect on her ultimate "why" the next time she's tempted to skip a workout: She wants to have enough energy to play with her children and ensure she's managing her health to live a long life. Remembering this strong intrinsic motivation can help her take action, even when it's tough. This approach can work for you, too.

DIRECTIONS

1. Grab a pen and paper or your notebook. Choose a goal that you're working toward and write it at the top of the page.

2. Now journal about your ultimate "why." Why is this goal something you care about? How does it relate to your values? Is there an element of intrinsic motivation that comes from within you?

3. Reflect on what you've written in the moments when motivation feels low.

Visualize How You'll Feel Afterward

Visualization is a powerful technique that can boost your motivation. There are countless days when I'm tempted to snooze my alarm and skip my morning walk, especially when I haven't slept well and have plenty of valid reasons for not going. However, I focus on the feeling I'm seeking from my walk. Before hitting snooze, I visualize how I will feel afterward—energized, clearheaded, calm, and ready to start my day. This desired feeling drives my behavior. Remembering how great I've felt after previous walks helps motivate me to get up and go.

DIRECTIONS

1. The next time you're tempted to put off something that's beneficial to your health, home, relationships, or career, pause wherever you are and sit down for a few moments.

2. Close your eyes and visualize how you'll feel after taking that action. Imagine the relief, sense of accomplishment, energy, and satisfaction you'll feel once you have performed that action.

3. Let that feeling drive you toward taking the beneficial action.

Improve Your Self-Talk

You can't blame, shame, or criticize yourself into making change. If this were effective, it would have worked by now. Instead, treat yourself with compassion throughout the process of change. When I work with clients who struggle with motivation, they often say things like "I'm so lazy," "I just can't do it," or "What's wrong with me? Why can't I ever do what I say I want to do?" This negative self-talk only makes it harder to change. Guilt, shame, and criticism are not effective long-term motivators. Extending compassion toward yourself when motivation is low will help you far more than self-criticism ever will.

DIRECTIONS

1. When you're struggling to take action, pay attention to what you are saying to yourself.

2. Grab a pen and paper or your notebook, and write out this internal dialogue in as much detail as possible.

3. Ask yourself, "What would I say to a friend who was speaking to themselves this way?" Write down some compassionate responses to each comment.

4. Now say your compassionate responses aloud to yourself. Notice how you feel.

5. If the critical voice continues to come up, keep challenging it with compassionate responses. For some more help with this, read the strategies covered in the "Inner Critic" guide on page 62.

Additional CBT Tools

The following guides may also be helpful if you're struggling with low motivation:

* ADHD (page 34)
* Depression (page 51)
* Guilt (page 118)
* Inner Critic (page 62)
* Procrastination (page 166)
* Sadness (page 125)
* Shame (page 134)

In addition, these CBT skills may also be useful:

* Avoid All-or-Nothing Thinking (page 175)
* Behavioral Activation (page 55)
* Eisenhower Matrix (page 37)
* Five-Minute Rule (page 36)
* Gamify Your Tasks (page 40)
* Identify Triggers and Cope Ahead (page 176)
* Limit Distractions (page 39)
* Pomodoro Timer (page 171)
* Predict Time and Difficulty (page 167)
* Set Realistic Expectations (page 169)
* Set Timers (page 41)
* Start Small with Manageable Goals (page 177)
* Thought Record (page 25)

Low Confidence

Confidence is your belief in yourself and your ability to overcome life's challenges. When you have a strong sense of self-confidence, you're generally better equipped to handle external pressure and overcome obstacles.

Many people have misconceptions about confidence that can make them feel defeated and doubt their ability to develop it. Here are two major misconceptions:

Confidence is innate. Some believe that confidence is an innate trait—you're either born with it or not. In reality, confidence can be cultivated over time, which is encouraging for those struggling with low confidence.

Confidence precedes action. Another misconception is that confidence must come before action. However, confidence is built by taking action. For example, a confident public speaker didn't start out commanding stages effortlessly; they cultivated their confidence through practice and experience.

If you struggle with low self-confidence, you likely lack belief in yourself, which can prevent you from taking risks and pursuing things that matter to you. If this is your challenge, you might:

THINK	FEEL	ACT
"I'll never be able to do that." "I'll never get there." "That's not possible for me." "I'm so bad at this." "This is too hard."	A sense of self-doubt Afraid to take risks Stuck and stagnant in your life Sad or depressed Hopeless about achieving your goals	Avoid taking risks Overplan and overprepare Keep yourself small Hide or shy away from others who make you doubt yourself

CBT can help you understand how your beliefs about yourself and your abilities contribute to your level of confidence. CBT also encourages you to give yourself opportunities to increase your confidence by taking risks, building mastery, and feeling more capable of handling life's challenges.

Combat Comparison

In my work with clients, I've seen that those who compare themselves to others are more likely to have low self-confidence. It's easy to focus on what others have or their achievements while downplaying your own. These unfair comparisons are a form of cognitive distortion, as discussed on page 17. In today's society, social media fosters a culture of comparison, which can harm our self-esteem. Comparisons that lead to low self-confidence might sound like:

* "She is so much prettier than I am."
* "My peers make so much more money than I do."
* "My coworker is so much smarter than I am. That must be why he got that raise."
* "My brother is so much more successful than I am."

While it's natural to compare yourself to others, being aware of these thoughts is a crucial first step. Identifying your triggers can also help you manage these feelings. For instance, you might compare yourself to others when browsing social media, working out at the gym, or shopping. Knowing your triggers allows you to either limit exposure to them or practice mindful awareness.

DIRECTIONS

1. Grab a pen and paper or your notebook. Think about what you are doing when you start unfairly comparing yourself to others. These are your triggers. List as many as come to mind.

2. Think about each of those triggering activities. What comparison thoughts do you have in those moments? Write them down, too.

3. Use tools from this book to work through these thoughts. You might complete a Thought Record (page 25), try Thought Defusion Techniques (page 85), Practice Self-Compassion (page 67), or use other exercises in this book.

Do a Strengths Inventory

If you struggle with low self-confidence, you might focus more on your weaknesses than on your strengths. A Strengths Inventory takes into account your accomplishments and talents, helping you recognize and appreciate your abilities for a more balanced view of yourself. Set aside 20 minutes for this exercise.

DIRECTIONS

1. Grab a pen and paper or your notebook. Write "Strengths Inventory" at the top of the page. Using as many pages as necessary to fully inventory your strengths, include labeled sections for the following: (1) accomplishments, (2) areas of competence, (3) intelligence, (4) creativity, (5) relationships, and (6) personality.

2. Under "Accomplishments," describe what you are proud of, big or small. Think beyond academics and career.

3. Under "Areas of Competence," describe what you are skilled at, what you do well, and what hobbies you enjoy.

4. Under "Intelligence," describe your knowledge and skills in any areas or tasks in which you feel confident in your abilities.

5. Under "Creativity," describe any creative interests or hobbies you like to participate in. Keep in mind that creativity can be less mainstream than art and music.

6. Under "Relationships," list the positive qualities those who care about you might mention if asked. Describe the positive qualities you bring to others as a partner, friend, family member, colleague, etc.

7. Under "Personality," list the traits others tend to admire in you. Describe the qualities you possess that attract others to you. For example, are you trustworthy, kind, respectful, understanding, etc.?

8. Review your finished inventory and notice how you feel. Has your mood shifted? What body sensations are you experiencing? It's normal to feel resistance, but with practice, you'll become more comfortable acknowledging your strengths.

9. Save your Strengths Inventory somewhere you can refer to in the future.

Create a Credits List

If you find it hard to give yourself credit, a Credits List can help. This exercise encourages you to recognize daily achievements, boosting your self-image. Since the idea is to keep adding to this list, it's a good idea to use a notebook to keep the list in one place.

DIRECTIONS

1. Grab a pen and paper or your notebook. Write "Credits List" at the top of the page.

2. Ask yourself, "What did I do today that I deserve credit for?" Include anything that felt challenging but you accomplished anyway. For example, if you're struggling with depression and found it difficult to get up and go to work but you did it anyway, then include that. If you're struggling with ADHD and accomplished a small task that you've been putting off, include that. Try to include at least three things.

3. Reflect on how you feel after you give yourself credit for these things. Notice any changes in how you feel or think about yourself.

4. Each day, spend three to five minutes adding at least three items to your Credits List.

Build Mastery

Building self-mastery is a dialectical behavior therapy (DBT) skill that challenges you to improve yourself so you feel less helpless. Developing self-mastery is key to increasing your self-confidence. Without it, you may feel powerless, doubt your ability to reach your goals, and believe that your efforts will not lead to your intended outcome. This keeps you from putting forth effort and working toward the things you want in life. By building self-mastery, you'll gather evidence to support the new belief that you are capable and can handle future challenging obstacles.

DIRECTIONS

1. Review the following ways to build mastery and, on a piece of paper or in your notebook, brainstorm a few actions you could take in each category:

    *   Do something that challenges you.

    *   Learn a new hobby or skill.

    *   Work toward a long-term goal.

    *   Make commitments to yourself and follow through.

2. Choose one of the actions you identified—and do it. For example, challenge yourself by going for a bike ride, starting a beginner's course on the piano, taking the first step in a bigger project, or committing to doing one exercise each day in this book.

3. Each time you take one of these actions, add it to your Credits List (see page 81). This will reinforce your confidence in your abilities and support your belief that you can achieve what you set your mind to.

Additional CBT Tools

The following guides may also be helpful if you're struggling with low confidence:

* Depression (page 51)
* Guilt (page 118)
* Inner Critic (page 62)
* Perfectionism (page 93)
* Sadness (page 125)
* Shame (page 134)

In addition, these CBT skills may also be useful:

* Challenge Rules and Assumptions (page 97)
* Challenge Your "Positive" Beliefs About Self-Criticism (page 65)
* Get to Know Your Inner Critic (page 64)
* Improve Your Self-Talk (page 75)
* Practice Self-Acceptance and Self-Compassion (page 139)
* Practice Self-Compassion (page 67)
* Thought Record (page 25)

Overthinking

Overthinking can appear in various forms, such as worry, rumination, and catastrophizing. Worry focuses on future uncertainties, rumination dwells on past events, and catastrophizing jumps to the worst-possible outcomes in any situation.

Overthinking might manifest as:

* Second-guessing your decisions
* Jumping to worst-case scenarios
* Dwelling on past events
* Replaying uncomfortable conversations
* Planning every minor detail
* Making lists to keep everything in order
* Trouble sleeping due to racing thoughts

Overthinking is your brain's way of trying to keep you safe and in control. While it might offer a false sense of security, letting go of overthinking can be liberating. Initially, it may feel scary to relinquish control, but it leads to long-term freedom.

CBT teaches you tangible tools to help you effectively combat overthinking and learn to trust yourself more. Trying to suppress unwanted thoughts only makes them persist. Instead, you'll learn to become a mindful observer of your thoughts. It might seem counterintuitive, but allowing your thoughts to be present helps them pass more quickly. Recognize that you are separate from your thoughts. Create distance using your breath and visualization techniques, and then let your thoughts float in and out of your mind with ease.

Depending on what you might need support with, there are specific techniques for rumination, worry, and catastrophizing.

Thought Defusion Techniques

ACT introduces thought defusion techniques to help you develop a mindful relationship with your thoughts. By practicing these techniques, you can create distance between yourself and your thoughts, allowing you to become a mindful observer. Some of the thought defusion techniques are more playful in nature, while others are more mindful. Over time, you'll begin to see which ones work well for you in the moment.

The core principles of thought defusion include:

* Not all thoughts are true or reflect reality.
* Not all thoughts need to carry significant weight.
* You are not your thoughts.

These insights help you recognize that thoughts are just thoughts, not facts, and you can choose how much attention and importance to give them.

DIRECTIONS

1. The next time you notice yourself overthinking, practice one of the following thought defusion techniques to stop the spiral of anxious thought:

   * Simply say, "I'm having the thought that . . ."
   * Thank your mind for having that thought and trying to keep you safe.
   * Visualize your thoughts like clouds floating in the sky.
   * Say the thought in a silly voice or sing it.
   * Take a step back and look at the thought from your observing self.
   * Imagine that your thoughts are like boxes on a conveyor belt.
   * Practice noticing. Simply notice what your mind is telling you right now.

* Close your eyes and visualize the thought. How big is it? What shape and color is it?

* Ask yourself if the thought is true, helpful, or effective.

* Name the story. What story is the thought trying to tell you? When it comes up in the future, name it and say, "There's that story again."

2. Was the technique successful? If so, great. If not, try another or several.

3. Continue to experiment with the various techniques to see which ones resonate with you and are most helpful.

Designated Worry Time

Designated worry time is a research-backed CBT technique designed to help you manage and reduce worry. By setting aside 5 to 10 minutes each night specifically for worrying, you can prevent worries from consuming your day and address them in a more controlled manner. This technique also helps you distinguish between productive and unproductive worries.

Letting go of worrying involves relinquishing control, which can be daunting. However, with practice, you will learn to trust yourself and the natural course of events.

DIRECTIONS

1. Throughout the day, notice any worries that arise. List them in your notebook or the notes section on your phone as they come up.

2. Avoid indulging in the worry at that moment. Commit to revisiting it during your designated worry time.

3. Schedule 10 minutes to complete this exercise each evening. When your worry time begins, set a timer for 5 minutes. Write down all your worries without holding back.

4. After the timer goes off, review your worries and consider:

   * What are the common themes in my worries?

   * What are the advantages and disadvantages of worrying about this?

   * Are my worries productive or unproductive? (Productive worries are those you can act on immediately, while unproductive worries cannot be addressed at the moment.)

   * Are there any actions I can take to address my current worries? If not, what must I work on accepting about the current situation?

5. End this designated worry time with a brief ritual that marks the end of the session. You could do something physical like go for a walk, use your hands to make food, or take slow, deep breaths. You could even write your worries on a piece of paper and then rip up that paper as a form of release.

6. Continue to practice releasing what is beyond your control, and you will find greater peace and confidence in handling life's uncertainties.

CBT TOOL

Grounding Techniques

Overthinking can leave you feeling stuck in your head, disconnected from the present moment. Grounding techniques help you reconnect to your body and orient you to the here and now, cultivating a sense of safety within your nervous system. There are three major ways in which we practice grounding: exteroceptive grounding through the senses, proprioceptive grounding (sensing where your body begins and ends in space), and awakening sensation in the body.

DIRECTIONS

1. Practice one or more of the following grounding techniques the next time you feel as though you can't stop thinking:

   * Place one hand on your heart and one hand on your belly.

   * Run warm water over your hands.

   * Dig your heels into the floor.

   * Push your hands against each other or rub them together.

   * Feel the weight of your body on the chair beneath you.

   * Look around and describe your environment in detail.

   * Notice and name all the sounds you can hear.

   * Carry a grounding object with you that you can hold.

   * Eat something and describe the flavors you taste.

   * Count backward from 100 to 1 to disrupt your current thought pattern.

2. Experiment with the various grounding methods to see which ones you find the most effective.

3. Continue to practice as needed.

Best, Worst, Most Realistic Outcome

Worrying about elaborate worst-case scenarios is your brain's way of trying to keep you safe and prepared in case something goes wrong. However, fixating on potential negative outcomes can keep you stuck in fear and stop you from taking action. This exercise encourages you to consider other potential outcomes. By doing so, you can:

> * **Reinforce realistic thinking.** You will assess threats more accurately because you understand that the most realistic scenario likely falls somewhere between the two extremes.
> * **Strengthen coping skills.** You will boost your confidence in your ability to cope and use problem-solving skills effectively.

DIRECTIONS

1. Notice when you are catastrophizing. When you catch yourself jumping to the worst-possible outcome, acknowledge it by saying, "I'm jumping to the worst-case scenario."

2. Then, with the current situation in mind, ask yourself:

    * What's the worst-case scenario?

    * What's the best-case scenario?

    * What's the most-realistic-case scenario?

3. Notice how reflecting on these questions helps you put things into perspective.

Mindfulness of Thoughts Meditation

Holding space for difficult thoughts and working through them requires gentleness and curiosity. Often, we judge our thoughts and try to suppress them. But what if we invited our thoughts in with gentle curiosity instead? Practicing mindfulness of thoughts means:

* Meeting your thoughts with curiosity in the moment
* Refraining from judging what you're thinking
* Noticing what thoughts are going through your mind in the moment
* Welcoming in your thoughts instead of suppressing them
* Visualizing your thoughts like clouds in the sky
* Being aware of how certain thoughts make you feel
* Separating your sense of self from your thoughts
* Knowing that not all thoughts are true
* Letting thoughts freely float in and out of your mind

DIRECTIONS

1. Sit or lie in a comfortable position and close your eyes. Begin to deepen your breath.

2. Visualize your thoughts like clouds floating by in the sky. Each time you notice a new thought, visualize placing it in a cloud and watch it gently float by.

3. Continue this practice for 5 to 10 minutes, observing each thought without judgment and letting it pass by like a cloud.

Additional CBT Tools

The following guides may also be helpful if you're struggling with overthinking:

* Anxiety (page 22)
* Chronic Stress (page 43)
* Fear (page 112)
* Inner Critic (page 62)
* Insomnia (page 151)
* People-Pleasing (page 159)
* Perfectionism (page 93)

In addition, these CBT skills may also be useful:

* Exposure Exercise (page 30)
* Exposure Hierarchy (page 28)
* Practice Mindfulness and Body-Based Techniques (page 48)
* Practice Self-Compassion (page 67)
* Thought Record (page 25)

Perfectionism

Perfectionism goes beyond simply wanting to be perfect. It involves constantly striving for unrealistic standards and basing your self-worth on whether you meet those standards. This often leads to a cycle of never feeling satisfied, as you continually raise the bar for yourself. Perfectionism can affect various aspects of your life, including school, work, appearance, fitness, and relationships.

Here are some indicators that perfectionism might be holding you back:

* You feel your best is never good enough.
* Achieving your goals only leads to setting even higher standards.
* You adopt an all-or-nothing approach to your objectives.
* Your inner critic is particularly harsh.
* Fear of imperfection causes you to procrastinate or avoid tasks.
* You notice your own mistakes, even when others don't.

Recognizing these signs is the first step toward overcoming perfectionism and embracing a more fulfilling and balanced life.

If you are struggling with perfectionism, you might:

THINK	FEEL	ACT
"I'm not allowed to make any mistakes. There's no room for mistakes."	Disappointed in yourself when you make a mistake	Beat yourself up when you make mistakes
"I must do everything perfectly."	Frustrated when you don't meet the standards you set for yourself	Speak to yourself in a harsh tone
"I'm a total failure."		Have trouble identifying your strengths
"I always hold myself to a high standard."	Pressure to always do things perfectly	Procrastinate when you feel the pressure for things to be done perfectly
"I must be good at this right away."	Paralyzed by fear when tasks seem daunting	
"If I don't do this perfectly, I might as well not even try."	Drained from trying so hard all the time	Constantly check and recheck for potential errors
"If I'm imperfect, others might reject me."	Afraid of failure, rejection, or abandonment	Try to make it seem like you "have it all together"

HOW DOES PERFECTIONISM DEVELOP?

Perfectionism often stems from childhood coping mechanisms. Many who struggle with it today developed these tendencies early on as a way to feel safe and gain approval. As children, they might have been praised only for high performance or felt love was conditional on their behavior. This led them to control and achieve as a means of coping.

As adults, these perfectionist tendencies can be more harmful than helpful. High performance is often praised, reinforcing these behaviors and making them hard to break. Understanding the origins of your perfectionism and showing compassion to your younger self can help you develop healthier coping mechanisms.

Healing begins by affirming your inner child with unconditional love, regardless of achievements.

Setting unrealistic standards and engaging in perfectionist thinking patterns perpetuate the cycle of perfectionism. These patterns include:

All-or-nothing thinking: View outcomes as either perfect or total failures, with no middle ground.

Should statements: Create rigid rules for yourself that you feel must be met to be worthy or accepted.

Magnification/minimization: Focus on negatives and downplay positives. There are common thought patterns and corresponding behaviors that are strongly associated with perfectionism. CBT can help you unravel your unhelpful beliefs about perfectionism, learn to set realistic standards for yourself, and encourage you to take imperfect action.

Bring Awareness to Your Perfectionism

Given perfectionism's deep roots, it's beneficial to explore how it affects you today. Reflect on the following questions and journal your responses on a sheet of paper or in your notebook:

* How does perfectionism show up in my daily life?
* When did I first notice my perfectionist tendencies?
* What high standards do I hold myself to? Are any of these standards unrealistic?
* How does perfectionism hold me back?
* How has my perfectionism been reinforced over time?
* How does perfectionism relate to my sense of self?
* What would I tell my inner child, who felt they had to be perfect to be loved?
* What am I afraid would happen if I let go of perfectionism?
* What small behavior changes can I make to challenge my perfectionism?
* How can I show myself compassion when I make mistakes?

CBT TOOL

Challenge Rules and Assumptions

Automatic thoughts are essentially your stream-of-consciousness, surface-level thoughts in any given moment. They are the most basic level of cognition in CBT. Beneath these thoughts lie deeper cognitive layers—what we call rules and underlying assumptions. Rules often manifest as "should" or "must" statements, while underlying assumptions typically take the form of "if-then" statements. These subconscious guidelines can influence your behavior and self-perception without your even realizing it. Here, you'll specifically identify and challenge your perfectionist rules and assumptions, but this can be used with any rules and assumptions you may have.

DIRECTIONS

1. Set aside 15 minutes to complete this exercise. Grab a pen and paper or your notebook.

2. What are some of your perfectionist rules and assumptions? Here are some examples:

    * "I must not make any mistakes at work."

    * "I have to do things perfectly on the first try."

    * "If I don't do this perfectly, then I might as well not even try."

    * "If I'm not perfect, I'll be rejected."

3. Of these rules and assumptions, which ones do you want to challenge? Respond to the following in writing:

    * What is the perfectionist rule or assumption I want to challenge?

    * How has this rule or assumption impacted my daily life?

    * Where did I learn this rule or assumption?

    * In what ways has this rule or assumption benefited or protected me?

* In what ways has this rule or assumption hurt me?

* How is this rule or assumption unreasonable? Do I hold others to this same rule?

* What am I afraid will happen if I let this rule or assumption go?

4. Think about a new rule or assumption that is more balanced, flexible, and supportive. Here are some examples:

* "I'm only human. It's okay to make mistakes."

* "It's okay to try something new and not be great at it right away. I can learn and grow over time."

* "It's better to do something imperfectly than to not do it at all."

* "Imperfection and vulnerability may actually help me get closer to other people and deepen our connection."

5. Think about ways you can begin to put this new belief into practice. Jot down your ideas. You may not immediately believe these new statements on an emotional level, but practicing them behaviorally will help you internalize these more supportive beliefs. Over time, you will see that it is safe to embrace imperfection.

Behavioral Experiment

Healing from perfectionism requires taking messy, imperfect action. This is the only way to truly see that it's safe to change your behaviors and embrace imperfection, however you define it.

DIRECTIONS

1. Identify a perfectionistic behavior you want to change. Be specific about what you plan to practice. Here are some practical ideas to get you started:

    *   Limit the time you spend on writing emails and texts.

    *   Speak freely without self-monitoring.

    *   Learn something new you've never tried before.

    *   Spend less time getting ready in the morning.

    *   Share how you're feeling with someone to let yourself be vulnerable and human.

    *   Admit when you don't know something and ask a question.

    *   Stop pretending you "have it all together."

    *   Embark on a creative project simply for fun.

2. Note your predictions. What do you think will happen if you carry out this experiment?

3. Decide when and where you will practice this behavior during the week. At the appointed place and time, carry out the behavior.

4. Afterward, consider whether your predictions came true. Did things turn out differently than you expected? What did you learn? How can you continue practicing this new behavior?

Additional CBT Tools

The following guides may also be helpful if you're struggling with perfectionism:

* Anxiety (page 22)
* Chronic Stress (page 43)
* Fear (page 112)
* Inner Critic (page 62)
* Insomnia (page 151)
* Low Confidence (page 77)
* People-Pleasing (page 159)
* Procrastination (page 166)

In addition, these CBT skills may also be useful:

* Challenge Your "Positive" Beliefs About Self-Criticism (page 65)
* Combat Comparison (page 79)
* Create a Credits List (page 81)
* Do a Strengths Inventory (page 80)
* Get to Know Your Inner Critic (page 64)
* Graded Tasks (page 71)
* Practice Self-Compassion (page 67)
* Thought Record (page 25)

CHAPTER 4

Regulate Your Emotions

Anger

Anger arises when something gets in the way of a desired outcome or when we believe there's been a violation of how things should be. It exists on a spectrum from annoyance to anger and potentially to rage. Unlike some emotions, anger can quickly intensify and manifest strongly in the body, often demanding outward expression due to its strong action urges.

Your relationship with anger is likely shaped by what you observed growing up. Ask yourself these questions to better understand your connection with anger:

* Did I witness extreme expressions of anger in my household?
* Was anger considered an acceptable or unacceptable emotion?
* Was anger used to mask other deeper emotions?
* How did others respond to me when I displayed feelings of anger?

There is ongoing debate among researchers about whether anger is a primary or secondary emotion. Sometimes, anger masks deeper, more uncomfortable emotions like hurt, rejection, or disappointment. Have you expressed anger but deep down felt hurt, rejected, or disappointed? If so, you've experienced firsthand how anger can be used to cover up more deeply rooted emotions. For example, maybe you were angry because you were passed over for a promotion, but then you dig a layer deeper and realize there's a lot of hurt and sadness there. You may feel like your best is never good enough or your value at work is not recognized.

CBT can help you identify your anger triggers, evaluate the need to act on your anger, and give you techniques to release the emotion from your physical body. Identifying your anger triggers allows you to cope ahead with situations that might bring up the feeling for you so that it doesn't intensify, which can happen quickly in the moment without strategies in place.

Anger Iceberg

The anger iceberg is a visual tool that helps illustrate the depth and complexity of anger. Anger is often just the tip of the iceberg—an emotion that is easy to identify. However, beneath the surface, similar to the massive bulk of an iceberg submerged in water, lie many other emotions that fuel the anger (see figure 4.1).

Figure 4.1: Anger Iceberg. This illustrates the many other emotions that can be underneath the surface of anger.

Emotions that might exist beneath the anger that fuel it include sadness, disappointment, jealousy, hurt, pain, fear, guilt, shame, and embarrassment. In that sense, anger acts as a mask to these more deeply rooted emotions. Depending on your relationship with anger and how it was modeled to you, you may find anger more comfortable or more acceptable, using it to subconsciously mask other emotions.

Identifying which emotions might live beneath your anger can help you nurture those primary emotions, getting to the root of the problem. If you uncover other emotions beneath your anger, you can reference the other guides in this book on sadness, fear, guilt, and shame.

DIRECTIONS

1. The next time you feel anger coming on, observe what emotions might be beneath the surface.

2. Give these emotions a name, such as "This is hurt," or "This is shame."

3. Practice validating the part of you that feels these emotions and meet that part with compassion. (See the Validate Your Feelings tool on page 127.)

4. Notice how acknowledging and validating these underlying emotions begins to shift the anger on the surface.

Identify Anger Triggers

If you often find yourself struggling with anger, identifying your triggers can be a helpful first step. Knowing what sets off your anger allows you to plan ahead and manage these moments more effectively. Triggers can come from various sources, such as people, environments, situations, emotions, or even specific thoughts.

DIRECTIONS

1. Identify your triggers. On a piece of paper or in your notebook, list people, environments, situations, other emotions, and thoughts that tend to trigger anger for you. Here are some examples:

    *   People: a distant relative, a coworker, a roommate, or an ex-partner

    *   Environments: your childhood home or a bar

    *   Situations: getting cut off in traffic, receiving feedback at work, or when your partner doesn't pick up after themselves

    *   Emotions: disappointment, hurt, or confusion

    *   Thoughts: "This is so stupid," "He's such an idiot," or "This is a massive inconvenience."

2. When the trigger is more within your control, cope ahead. Outline your strategy for avoiding or reducing exposure to each trigger. Here are some examples:

    *   If a coworker triggers you, request to do more projects with someone else on your team.

    *   If visiting your childhood home is a trigger, make plans to get together with your family in a neutral setting.

    *   If your thoughts trigger you, notice if there's a cognitive distortion and work to reframe the thought (see page 175).

3. If the trigger cannot be avoided, approach the anger head-on. Outline your strategy for dealing with each trigger. Here are some examples:

* If getting cut off in traffic triggers you, try to take that situation less personally by acknowledging that, although it was rude, the other driver didn't intentionally target you.

* If unavoidable emotions such as disappointment, hurt, or confusion trigger you, try to meet yourself with compassion and address your primary emotions in the moment. For example, "It's okay to feel hurt by *(fill in the blank)*."

* If you have to attend a family gathering with a relative who triggers you, practice cultivating empathy, but also take breaks as needed.w

How to Respond to Anger Behaviorally

Anger often arises quickly and seeks outward expression. It may make you want to lash out, criticize, attack, or yell. Acting on these urges can harm your relationships and even intensify your feelings. Understanding how your behaviors fit into the cognitive model and deciding whether acting on a particular emotion will serve you are essential. If you realize that expressing your anger immediately won't benefit you or others, you can choose to respond differently. This intentional choice can help you feel better overall.

Instead of lashing out, consider taking a brief time-out, gently avoiding the person you are angry with, cultivating empathy, or taking deep breaths to calm your nervous system. In some situations, it might be beneficial to channel your anger into assertiveness and set boundaries.

DIRECTIONS

1. Practice observing the early warning signs of anger in your body. Notice, for example, when your face feels hot, your heart rate elevates, you feel tension in your stomach or chest, or your muscles get tight.

2. Label the emotion as anger in the moment.

3. Pause before you do anything else. Notice how the anger makes you want to behave in the moment and ask yourself:

    * Will it serve me or the other people involved to act on this emotion in this moment?

    * What can I do to help myself regulate in this moment? (See the Body-Based Techniques for Anger tool on page 110.)

    * Do I want to commit to returning to this situation and addressing it once I've cooled off?

4. Based on what you've concluded, respond accordingly. Practice acting in a way that will serve you, the situation, and the other people involved, especially if you value these relationships.

Body-Based Techniques for Anger

Anger often manifests strongly in the physical body. Your body's response to anger could include flushing, an elevated heart rate, stomach discomfort, sweating, and so on. Practicing somatic (body-based) techniques that allow you to move through that energy can be beneficial in the moment.

DIRECTIONS

1. When you notice your body reacting physically to anger, remove yourself from the situation and, if possible, go somewhere you can be alone for a few minutes.

2. Practice one of the following somatic techniques until you feel calm:

   * **Diaphragmatic breathing:** Take deep breaths, focusing on breathing from your diaphragm.

   * **Intense exercise:** Engage in a short, intense burst of exercise like running, jumping jacks, or burpees.

   * **Push a wall:** Place your hands on a solid wall and safely push against it.

   * **Progressive muscle relaxation:** Tense and release individual muscle groups. For example, squeeze your fists into tight balls as you inhale and then release the tension as you exhale. (See page 48.)

3. Check in with your body before and after to notice any physiological changes.

Additional CBT Tools

The following guides may also be helpful if you're struggling with anger:

* Chronic Stress (page 43)
* Depression (page 51)
* Guilt (page 118)
* Ineffective Communication (page 144)
* Sadness (page125)
* Shame (page 134)

In addition, these CBT skills may also be useful:

* Active Listening (page 145)
* Combat Mind Reading (page 149)
* Mindfulness of Emotions (page 129)
* Practice Assertive Communication (page 161)
* Practice Mindfulness and Body-Based Techniques (page 48)
* Practice Self-Acceptance and Self-Compassion (page 139)
* Respond Thoughtfully (page 146)
* Thought Record (page 25)
* Use "I" Statements (page 147)
* Validate Your Feelings (page 127)

Fear

Fear is triggered by real or perceived threats or danger, activating the brain's alarm system to motivate us to act quickly out of self-preservation. While fear and anxiety can feel similar, fear is a response to an immediate threat, while anxiety is focused on future events or situations. Common fears include things like spiders, rodents, snakes, heights, and the dark.

There are many situations that can trigger feelings of fear, including:

* Confronting an unfamiliar situation
* A threat to your safety
* Being in a situation where you've been hurt in the past
* Public speaking/performing in front of others
* Taking risks

In my work with clients, I've noticed a number of universal fears, including the fear of uncertainty, change, failure, rejection, and judgment, which more or less affect each of us to some degree. This guide focuses on addressing some of those universal fears.

CBT can help you identify your fear triggers and increase your awareness of your natural fear response. It also aids in understanding how your thoughts and interpretations of feared situations may intensify the feelings of fear you're experiencing. CBT encourages you to confront your fears to overcome them.

> **Note:** *Exposures and confronting fears head-on should not be applied to situations that are legitimately unsafe. Exposures are intended to help you overcome fears when your feelings may be out of proportion to the actual threat present.*

Locus of Control

Humans are hardwired to seek predictability and security. Not knowing what will happen in the future can trigger anxiety due to the lack of control and perceived safety. If you struggle intensely with a fear of uncertainty, you may worry excessively about the future, try to find ways to control outcomes, seek reassurance from others, and/or avoid taking risks or making major transitions in your life.

It's important to assess what's truly within your realm of control versus what's outside it. Developed by psychologist Julian Rotter, the Locus of Control exercise can help you see what's worth worrying over and what's worth releasing. Here's why this exercise works:

* You may realize there's more in your control than you initially thought, which can feel empowering.
* You are able to assess where your energy is best spent.
* You can clearly understand which aspects of the situation call for practicing acceptance.

Once you determine which factors are within your realm of control versus which ones are outside it, you can better assess where your focus, attention, and energy are best spent.

DIRECTIONS

1. In your notebook or on a piece of paper, describe the situation and your fears of uncertainty surrounding that situation. Use the example on page 114 as a guide.

2. Split the remainder of the page in half. Label the left side "Things Within My Control" and the right side "Things Outside My Control."

3. In the left column, list all the aspects of the situation that are within your realm of control.

4. In the right column, list all the aspects of the situation that fall outside your realm of control.

5. Carefully review your lists and practice focusing your energy on what you can control and releasing your grip on what you cannot control. Instead of wasting precious energy and mental resources focusing on the things you can't impact, shifting your focus to the things within your realm of control can empower you.

Situation and fears: *I'm in the process of applying for new jobs, and I'm struggling to manage the uncertainty about my future, what my new role will be, how long it may take for me to find the right fit, and how this new job will impact my life.*

THINGS WITHIN MY CONTROL	THINGS OUTSIDE MY CONTROL
How much time I spend researching positions	The number of open positions that are available
The quality of my application materials	Whether I receive a reply from people after reaching out
Which specific positions I choose to apply to	The quality and quantity of the other potential applicants
The number of positions I apply to	What the hiring managers are looking for specifically
Reaching out to people within my network	How long the process ends up taking until I find a new position
Following up with people after I've reached out	
Preparing for job interviews	
How I present myself during interviews	

How to Cope with the Fear of Rejection

As humans, we naturally seek acceptance and connection, so feeling rejected can be deeply painful. This fear can show up in our social lives, romantic relationships, and professional settings. If you find yourself intensely afraid of rejection, you might avoid social situations, shy away from taking risks, or become overly sensitive to criticism. However, avoiding these situations only reinforces the fear. The best way to overcome it is to face potential rejection and work through the thoughts and feelings that arise when it happens.

DIRECTIONS

1. In your notebook or on a piece of paper, identify a situation when you experienced rejection and felt pain as a result. Write out the specifics—who, what, when, and where. Stick to the facts.

2. Outline any thoughts or beliefs that were triggered by the rejection. Did your mind jump to any of the following (or similar) thoughts:

   * If you experienced romantic rejection, did you think, "They didn't want to go on a date with me because I'm unattractive," and/or "I'll be alone forever"?

   * If you experienced social rejection, did you think, "Nobody likes me," and/or "I'm such a loser"?

   * If you experienced career rejection, did you think, "I didn't get the job, so I must not be smart enough," and/or "I'm incapable"?

3. Challenge these beliefs. As you can see, it's not the rejection itself that is so painful, it's the storyline you attach to it and what you believe the rejection means about you. Ask yourself:

   * Is what I believe about myself true? Is there any evidence to suggest that these thoughts are untrue?

* Are there reasons I was rejected that have nothing to do with me? What are other factors that could have led to the outcome?

4. Write a new belief. What's a more supportive way of looking at this situation? The new belief might sound like:

   * "Even though I wasn't included for this social event, I have other people in my life who I know care about me and make an effort to include me."

   * "Even though I was turned down by this one person and that was painful, that doesn't mean I'll be alone forever. There are so many other people out there for me to connect with."

   * "Even though I was rejected from this job, I possess many strengths that I bring to the workplace."

5. Finally, normalize rejection and continue to expose yourself to it in the future. Continue to take risks and put yourself out there. Experiencing rejection is a normal part of the human experience. I feel that this reminder helps so many of my clients struggling with feelings of rejection. So many of us have gotten turned down by potential dates, received rejection letters from employers, or been left out from social gatherings.

6. This doesn't necessarily make it any less painful, but it can encourage you to take these moments of rejection less personally and challenge the belief that the rejection reflects something wrong or shameful about you. Practicing self-compassion in these moments goes a long way, too.

Note: *This exercise also helps with the fear of failure. Notice the storyline you attach to a perceived failure, shift your thinking around it, normalize failure as a part of the human experience, and continue to expose yourself to it over time.*

Additional CBT Tools

The following guides may also be helpful if you're struggling with fear:

* Anxiety (page 22)
* Inner Critic (page 62)
* Low Confidence (page 77)
* Perfectionism (page 93)
* Shame (page 134)

In addition, these CBT skills may also be useful:

* Best, Worst, Most Realistic Outcome (page 90)
* Designated Worry Time (page 87)
* Exposure Exercise (page 30)
* Exposure Hierarchy (page 28)
* Grounding Techniques (page 89)
* Mindfulness of Emotions (page 129)
* Mindfulness of Thoughts Meditation (page 91)
* Practice Mindfulness and Body-Based Techniques (page 48)
* Thought Defusion Techniques (page 85)
* Thought Record (page 25)
* Validate Your Feelings (page 127)

Guilt

Guilt is an emotion we feel when our actions conflict with our values. It often arises when we act out of character or hurt someone. This sense of guilt and regret can motivate us to apologize and make amends, making guilt a positive driver for behavior change compared to shame (see page 134). While guilt and shame often occur together, they are distinct emotions. Guilt arises when you believe you have done something wrong or bad. In contrast, shame is triggered by the belief that you, as a person, are inherently bad or wrong. Recognizing this difference is crucial for processing these emotions effectively and fostering a healthier self-view.

When processed effectively, guilt can inspire us to improve without unfairly beating ourselves up. Many scenarios can prompt feelings of guilt, such as:

Acting against your values: doing something you believe is wrong

Breaking promises: not following through on commitments

Causing harm: hurting others, intentionally or unintentionally

Past actions: remembering something regrettable you did in the past

In these situations, you might think, "I shouldn't have done that," or "That was out of character for me," which leads to feelings of guilt. However, it's important to recognize when guilt is unnecessary—when you unfairly blame yourself for something beyond your responsibility or control. This distinction is crucial, as it influences how you process guilt and move forward.

Situations that can prompt unwarranted feelings of guilt include:

* Leaving a job for a new opportunity to support your long-term career growth
* Spending time away from your children as a parent
* Setting a boundary or voicing your needs if you struggle with people-pleasing
* Resting and having downtime when there are still items on your to-do list
* Saying no to an invitation or an obligation when your plate is full

Situations that warrant guilt:

* Cheating on your romantic partner
* Breaking your friend's or loved one's trust
* Making fun of someone or acting in a mean way
* Acting out of character to get ahead
* Doing something you believe is wrong and against your values

Guilt is a strong driver of behavior. As the cognitive model outlines, guilt can lead us to specific behaviors. Typically, it drives us to apologize, seek forgiveness, and attempt to repair any harm we've caused. When managed appropriately, these actions can be positive outcomes of guilt. However, if guilt leads you to unfairly blame yourself, beat yourself up, or struggle with self-forgiveness, it can become toxic and more harmful than helpful. If this resonates with you, you may find the Participation Pie tool on page 121 and Practice Self-Forgiveness tool on page 123 particularly beneficial.

CBT offers effective techniques to manage feelings of guilt, depending on the nature of the situation. If your guilt is warranted and you wish to make amends, CBT can guide you through the process of apologizing and repairing any harm done. However, if you're unfairly blaming yourself, CBT provides tools such as the Participation Pie for unwarranted guilt on page 121. This technique helps you accurately assess your role in the situation, ensuring you don't shoulder unnecessary blame.

Apologize When Guilt Is Warranted

If you've done something that doesn't align with your values and hurt someone you care about, it's important to offer a sincere apology and attempt to make amends. Here are the steps of a sincere apology:

1. Do it for the right reasons.
2. Take responsibility. Acknowledge what you did wrong.
3. Express genuine regret and remorse.
4. Make amends. Ask how you can make it right.
5. Understand how the other person expects to be treated in the future.
6. Reaffirm the boundaries within your relationship with the other person.
7. Change your behavior accordingly. Actions speak louder than words.
8. Give the other person time and space to process.

DIRECTIONS

1. Grab a pen and paper or your notebook. As you prepare to offer an apology, reflect on the following:

   * What did I do?

   * Why was this hurtful?

   * How does this behavior violate my values?

   * How does this make me feel?

   * What do I want the other person to know?

   * How do I plan to change my behavior moving forward to honor the boundaries that exist in this relationship?

2. At a time that works for you and the other person, offer your sincere apology.

Participation Pie

The Participation Pie is a CBT technique that helps you manage feelings of guilt by developing a more balanced perspective on the causes of a particular event, especially when you unfairly blame yourself. This tool is useful for situations when you might think, "This was all my fault," or "I should have had the power to stop this bad thing from happening." The goal is not to shift blame but to recognize all contributing factors and people involved in the outcome.

For example, while escorting your elderly mother to your car, she falls and breaks her hip. Your immediate reaction is to blame yourself for the accident. However, once you outline all the contributing factors, you see that your mother's accident was not your sole responsibility. There were many factors that led to the unfortunate outcome. Your guilt in this situation is simply an indication of how much empathy you have for your mother and how much it pains you to see her experience this. Here's what your pie chart might look like:

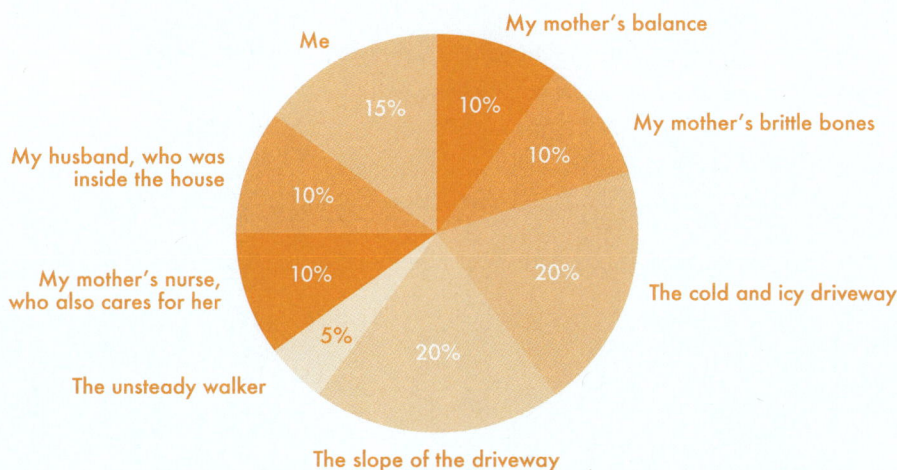

Figure 4.2: Participation Pie of Contributions to Mother's Accident

DIRECTIONS

1. Do a gut check. Write "I believe I am X percent guilty for X." There is no right or wrong answer. This will simply allow you to check in and compare your score at the start of the exercise to your score at the end of the exercise.

2. Draw a large circle in the middle of a blank page. This is 100 percent of the pie. On a separate page, list all the possible contributing factors, assigning each factor a percentage of the overall participation. Save yourself for last and assign yourself the remaining percentage. The percentage points should add up to 100 percent.

3. Draw slices in the pie as shown in the example, giving each factor its own percentage of space.

4. As you evaluate your Participation Pie, ask yourself:

   * Am I blaming myself for things outside my realm of control?

   * Would I blame someone else as harshly for the same thing?

   * Am I unfairly exaggerating my role in events?

5. Reflect on this exercise. What did you learn? How do you feel? Are you looking at the situation through a different lens?

6. Do another gut check. Write "I believe I am X percent guilty for X." Notice the shift in your ratings and how you feel as a result.

Practice Self-Forgiveness

After you complete the Participation Pie, there may still be a part of you that is resistant to letting go of guilt. It's not uncommon for people with high levels of unwarranted guilt to be those with excellent character and a strong moral compass. Often, these people have been conditioned to believe they must be perfect, always put others first, and be self-sacrificing. This conditioning can lead to a belief that they deserve punishment and that releasing guilt means letting themselves off the hook. However, holding on to guilt does not benefit anyone involved.

DIRECTIONS

1. When you recognize that you're struggling to let go of guilt and forgive yourself, grab a pen and paper or your notebook and take some time for yourself.

2. On a blank page, journal your responses to the following:

   * What's my relationship to the emotion of guilt?

   * Did I grow up in a household or culture where guilt and shame were used as tactics to control certain behaviors?

   * How do I believe guilt is serving me or others?

   * What part of me is resistant to letting the guilt go?

   * What do I fear if I were to let the guilt go?

   * What would it look like for me to begin to forgive myself? How would I feel?

> **Note:** *If you are working on offering yourself forgiveness, you will benefit from the Practice Self-Compassion tool on page 67.*

Additional CBT Tools

The following guides may also be helpful if you're struggling with guilt:

* Depression (page 51)
* Inner Critic (page 62)
* Low Confidence (page 77)
* People-Pleasing (page 159)
* Sadness (page 125)
* Shame (page 134)

In addition, these CBT skills may also be useful:

* Mindfulness of Emotions (page 129)
* Practice Assertive Communication (page 161)
* Practice Mindfulness and Body-Based Techniques (page 48)
* Practice Self-Acceptance and Self-Compassion (page 139)
* Share in Safe Spaces (page 140)
* Thought Record (page 25)
* Uncover Negative Core Beliefs (page 136)
* Validate Your Feelings (page 127)

Sadness

Sadness is a universal primary emotion that we all experience in response to loss. It's important to distinguish sadness from depression and grief, as each has its own characteristics. Sadness is a common reaction to loss, whereas depression is a more persistent and complex condition with multiple symptoms. Grief, while often involving sadness, is a multifaceted process that encompasses a range of emotions.

There are many situations that can trigger feelings of sadness:

* Losing something or someone
* Missing the way things once were
* Things not going as planned
* Being left out or rejected
* A relationship ending

When experiencing sadness, we often feel the urge to retreat and become inactive. This can manifest in behaviors such as withdrawing from social events, avoiding responsibilities, and losing interest in pleasurable activities. Physically, we may feel tired or low energy. There may be a lump in our throat, a pit in our stomach, or a desire to cry as a way of releasing.

So often, we suppress our uncomfortable emotions or invalidate ourselves when we're feeling low. We tell ourselves that we "should" feel differently or to "get over it." This only serves to make us feel worse. For that reason, this guide emphasizes a compassionate, mindful, and validating approach to processing feelings of sadness. Moreover, remaining inactive, withdrawing, and avoiding things can also intensify feelings of sadness.

CBT helps you identify the thoughts that lead to sadness and the behaviors that follow. By promoting mindfulness, CBT teaches you to process emotions effectively instead of suppressing them. If you experience persistent sadness, reading the "Depression" guide on page 51 can be particularly helpful. Practicing behavioral activation, for instance, can be beneficial if your sadness has led you to withdraw from others or stop engaging in activities you once enjoyed.

Validate Your Feelings

Do you often find yourself invalidating your feelings or thinking you shouldn't feel the way you do? This might stem from never learning emotional validation, having your emotions dismissed by caregivers, or being told you were too sensitive or dramatic. As an adult, developing the skill of self-validation is crucial for managing your emotions effectively.

Validating your emotions is the first step toward healthy emotional management. By becoming aware of and acknowledging your feelings, you can process them in a healthy way. Suppressing or ignoring emotions can cause them to build up and potentially manifest physically. Emotional validation also reduces the shame around your feelings and fosters self-compassion.

DIRECTIONS

1. The next time you're struggling with sadness or another difficult emotion, carve out time to sit with the emotion.

2. Pause. Take deep breaths. Place your hands over your heart.

3. Notice the emotion. Notice how you're feeling in this moment. Notice how it feels in your body.

4. Name the emotion. Say, "This is sadness," or "This is fear."

5. Allow the emotion to be present without resisting it.

6. Validate yourself. Grant yourself permission to feel the way that you do without judgment. Validating your own feelings sounds like:

   * "It's okay for me to feel how I'm feeling in this moment."

   * "My feelings are totally valid even if others don't understand."

   * "I bet someone else in this same situation would feel this way, too."

   * "This has been a really challenging time for me."

   * "My emotional reactions are based on my lived experiences."

* "I give myself full permission to feel all my feelings."

* "My feelings of disappointment show how much I cared about this situation."

7. Remind yourself that your emotional reactions are based on your lived experiences.

8. Don't try to justify or explain the reason for the emotion to others. Know that your emotions are valid even if others don't understand or tell you that you shouldn't feel that way.

CBT TOOL

Mindfulness of Emotions

It can be tempting to suppress or ignore uncomfortable emotions, especially if they feel intense. However, this only causes the emotions to build up over time. Instead, it's important to develop skills to process your emotions effectively, and practicing mindfulness can help.

Often, we judge emotions as good or bad, tell ourselves our feelings are unjustified, or push them away for later. What if we invited the emotion in with gentle curiosity instead? Practicing mindfulness of emotions means resisting the urge to label emotions as positive or negative, allowing them to be present in the moment, and letting them pass naturally. Practicing mindfulness of emotions involves:

* Meeting your emotions with curiosity in the moment
* Refraining from judging how you're feeling
* Noticing how different emotions feel in your body
* Welcoming your emotions instead of resisting them
* Understanding that no emotions are inherently positive or negative
* Remembering that emotions are like temporary visitors that will pass
* Separating your sense of self from your emotions
* Being present with any uncomfortable emotions or sensations
* Sitting in the seat of the mindful observer

DIRECTIONS

1. Find a comfortable position, either seated or lying down, and gently close your eyes. Start to deepen your breath, elongating your inhales and exhales. Begin to notice how you feel emotionally. Get curious about the feelings present in this moment and allow them to arise without pushing them away. Invite them in with curiosity.

2. Observe where you feel these emotions in your body. Give each emotion a name, such as "This is sadness" or "This is fear." Notice how it feels to acknowledge the emotion aloud. Grant yourself permission to feel whatever you are experiencing right now.

3. Practice being the mindful observer of your emotions. You're not attaching to them or getting swept up in them; you're simply observing and allowing the emotion to run its course. Continue to breathe deeply as you do this.

4. As the intensity of the emotion increases and washes over you, breathe and sit with it. Visualize the rise, peak, and crash of a wave as you experience the emotion. Notice how the sensations in your body begin to shift and the emotion starts to settle. Continue to breathe deeply.

5. When you're ready, gently open your eyes and look around the room to reorient yourself to your space.

Plan a Comforting Activity

If you find that your feelings of sadness are so intense that you're withdrawing, isolating yourself from others, and no longer engaging in activities that once gave you pleasure, you will benefit from practicing behavioral activation. Rather than acting in a way that might intensify the sadness you feel, behavioral activation encourages you to take deliberate action that may help lift your mood.

DIRECTIONS

1. Review the Behavioral Activation exercise on page 56 for guidance. However, it isn't necessary to track your activities for a whole week before you take action.

2. In your notebook or on a piece of paper, create a unique list of activities you feel might lighten your mood or bring you comfort.

3. Choose an activity and plan to do it in the next few days or even today.

Address Sadness-Related Cognitive Distortions

Working through feelings of sadness is really about validating the feelings and allowing yourself to process them and move through them rather than suppress them. But sometimes the meaning you attach to the emotions, such as sadness, can make you feel worse. You can work through this, too.

DIRECTIONS

1. The next time you begin to feel sad, notice how your mind interprets the emotion. In response to feelings of sadness, do you recognize any of these cognitive distortions:

    *   All-or-nothing thinking: "I'm going to feel this way forever."

    *   Magnification/catastrophizing: "I'm not capable of coping with this emotion."

    *   Shoulds: "I shouldn't be feeling this way. I should be over it by now."

    *   Underlying rule/assumption: "Sadness makes me weak."

2. If you recognize sadness-related cognitive distortions, flip to the Thought Record exercise on page 26 and follow the directions. If you feel your thoughts accurately match your feelings, simply be mindful of the emotion (see page 129).

Additional CBT Tools

The following guides may also be helpful if you're struggling with sadness:

* Depression (page 51)
* Guilt (page 118)
* Inner Critic (page 62)
* Lack of Motivation (page 69)
* Low Confidence (page 77)
* Shame (page 134)

In addition, these CBT skills may also be useful:

* Behavioral Activation (page 55)
* Practice Mindfulness and Body-Based Techniques (page 48)
* Practice Self-Compassion (page 67)
* Share in Safe Spaces (page 140)
* Thought Record (page 25)
* Wheel of Life (page 53)

Shame

Shame is a deeply rooted emotion. In *The Atlas of Emotions,* Brené Brown, one of the foremost researchers of shame, defines *shame* as "the intensely painful feeling or experience of believing that we are flawed and therefore, unworthy of love, belonging, and connection." She goes on to say, "Shame thrives on secrecy, silence, and judgment." Studies show that shame is strongly correlated with mental health conditions, including depression, addiction, and eating disorders.

There are many situations that can prompt feelings of shame, such as:

* Comparing yourself to a set standard and feeling as though you don't meet it
* Being criticized, attacked, or laughed at
* Experiencing rejection by a group or people you care about
* Believing that you have failed at something
* Having something personal about yourself or a perceived flaw be exposed

Each of these situations triggers beliefs about yourself and your value, which bring up feelings of shame. Shame is a powerful driver of behavior. According to the cognitive model, shame can influence you to act in specific ways, such as hiding, isolating yourself, keeping your head down, and keeping secrets about what you feel ashamed of. These behaviors, especially when shame is unwarranted, can perpetuate and intensify the feeling over time.

Guilt and shame often occur together, but they are distinct emotions. Guilt arises when you feel you have done something wrong, whereas shame stems from the belief that you, as a person, are bad or wrong.

CBT helps you to uncover your core beliefs about yourself. Often, negative core beliefs are steeped in shame. CBT offers tools to help you challenge these negative beliefs and strengthen more adaptive core beliefs about yourself. CBT also helps you to see the impact that shame has on your behaviors and choose to act in a way that minimizes shame.

Uncover Negative Core Beliefs

Core beliefs are the most deeply rooted layer of beliefs that exist beneath your automatic thoughts and underlying rules and assumptions. All three layers are interconnected. To get to the root, you'll be looking at your thoughts, feelings, and actions around a situation, what rules and assumptions you've made with regard to similar situations, and what lies beneath the surface of it all. This is part of the Downward Arrow Technique, which you'll learn in this exercise.

The core beliefs you hold about yourself were likely formed early in life and have been continually strengthened over time. This process occurs because when your brain has a preexisting belief, it collects evidence to further support this belief while distorting, discounting, or minimizing evidence that contradicts it. Often, these negative underlying core beliefs are steeped in shame.

Thankfully, it is possible to use behaviors to reduce the power of negative core beliefs and cultivate new, more positive ones. For example, if you struggle with the belief that you are incompetent, then you can seek out situations that give you the opportunity to reinforce the belief that you are, in fact, capable and competent. Doing things like learning new skills or taking on easy projects at work helps your brain internalize this belief.

CBT identifies three main classifications of core beliefs that account for most negative core beliefs: incompetence, unlovability, and worthlessness. Here's how each might sound:

INCOMPETENCE CORE BELIEFS	UNLOVABILITY CORE BELIEFS	WORTHLESSNESS CORE BELIEFS
"I'm such a failure."	"I'm unlovable."	"I'm not good enough."
"I'm incompetent."	"I'm undesirable."	"I'm worthless."
"I'm a loser."	"I'm unwanted."	"I'm a bad person."

1. Choose a recent situation that brought up strong feelings for you. On a piece of paper or in your notebook, outline the cognitive model associated with this situation:

   * Situation: Describe the event that triggered your emotional response.

   * Automatic Thoughts: Note the immediate thoughts that came to mind during the situation.

   * Emotions: Identify the emotions you felt in response to these thoughts.

   * Behaviors: Observe the actions you took as a result of these emotions and thoughts.

2. To do the Downward Arrow Technique, start with your automatic thought, as shown in the example on page 138. For example, if your automatic thought is "I can't believe I made that mistake at work," ask yourself, "If I made that mistake, what does that mean about me?" Answer the question honestly. For example, you may think, "It means I'm careless with my work."

3. Continue asking, "If that's true, what does that mean about me?" For example, "If I'm careless with my work, what does that mean about me?"

4. Keep going until you reach a core belief. Your core belief will usually be a broad, overarching statement about yourself, such as "I'm incompetent," "I'm unlovable," or "I'm worthless."

5. Once you've uncovered your core belief, take time to journal about it in your notebook and reflect on the origins of your core belief. Ask yourself:

   * When is the first time I believed this about myself? How old was I? What happened that made me believe this about myself?

   * Were there other people whose message made me believe this about myself?

   * How has this belief been further strengthened over time?

   * How has this belief impacted my life?

   * Am I ready to let go of this old core belief?

* What more adaptive core belief would I like to work on strengthening?

* What evidence is there to support my old core belief?

* What evidence is there to support my new core belief?

EXAMPLE OF THE DOWNWARD ARROW TECHNIQUE

Automatic thought: "I can't believe I made that mistake at work." . . .
If I made that mistake, what does that mean about me?

↓

"It means that I'm careless with my work." . . .
If I'm careless with my work, what does that mean about me?

↓

"It means that I might lose my job and not be able to find a new one." . . .
If I lose my job and might not be able to find a new one, what does that
mean about me?

↓

"I'm incompetent." (This is my core belief.)

CBT TOOL

Practice Self-Acceptance and Self-Compassion

Uncovering the origin of your core belief allows you to identify the moment when you first felt that way about yourself. For example, if your core belief is "I'm undesirable," you might recall feeling left out on the playground, being rejected by someone you liked, or having a parent point out a perceived flaw. Recognizing these moments can be the first step toward healing and transforming your beliefs. This practice will help you not only believe on a cognitive level that there is nothing inherently wrong or flawed about you but also, and more important, truly feel that emotionally on a deeper level.

DIRECTIONS

1. Visualize the part of you that first believed your core belief to be true. Bring to mind as many details as you can. Notice how that part of you feels. Maybe it's a sense of shame, embarrassment, or sadness.

2. Place your hands over your heart or belly and take slow deep breaths as you cultivate compassion for this part of you.

3. Extend compassion to this part of you and tell it what it needs to hear: "I see you. I feel for you. There is nothing wrong with you."

4. Be present with whatever emotions surface. Working through core beliefs and connecting with younger parts of you can bring up deep emotions.

5. Continue to breathe and stick with this visual for as long as you need.

6. Check in with your physical body to notice any shifts or changes that may have occurred throughout that exercise. Notice how you feel.

Share in Safe Spaces

Shame often makes you want to hide, isolate, and keep your feelings secret, which can intensify the shame you feel. However, opening up and practicing vulnerability can help diminish shame. When you are met with acceptance rather than judgment, you may start to think, "Maybe it is okay to share this part of myself with others," and begin to feel less shame.

For example, I work with many clients struggling with social anxiety who often feel ashamed about having social anxiety. They worry about being judged as weird or strange, which prevents them from sharing openly. This secrecy reinforces the idea that social anxiety is something to be ashamed of. In group therapy, when these clients share their experiences with others facing similar struggles, their feelings of shame begin to lift. They realize they are not alone and that there is nothing wrong with them.

DIRECTIONS

1. Identify what you feel shameful about that you're tempted to keep hidden from others. Is it a past traumatic event, a failed relationship, getting fired from a job, an addiction, or something about your personality?

2. Seek out safe spaces to slowly open up and practice vulnerability. Start by considering who in your life is a safe person. Who has demonstrated empathy and emotional intelligence? Who has proven that they are nonjudgmental and a good listener? Begin to open up to such people through honest dialogue. That might mean you share something you're struggling with emotionally or a recent loss you've experienced.

3. If you do not have someone in your life who you feel is a safe person, seek out a group or someone who can play this role for you. This might mean that you seek out a therapist or a support group. Sharing openly and honestly with others who can relate helps to slowly lessen the feelings of shame over time.

Additional CBT Tools

The following guides may also be helpful if you're struggling with shame:

* Depression (page 51)
* Guilt (page 118)
* Inner Critic (page 62)
* Low Confidence (page 77)
* Sadness (page 125)

In addition, these CBT skills may also be useful:

* Apologize When Guilt Is Warranted (page 120)
* Build Mastery (page 82)
* Challenge Your "Positive" Beliefs About Self-Criticism (page 65)
* Combat Comparison (page 79)
* Create a Credits List (page 81)
* Do a Strengths Inventory (page 80)
* Get to Know Your Inner Critic (page 64)
* Mindfulness of Emotions (page 129)
* Participation Pie (page 121)
* Practice Self-Compassion (page 67)
* Practice Self-Forgiveness (page 123)
* Thought Record (page 25)

CHAPTER FIVE

Change Your Behaviors

Ineffective Communication

It can be challenging to communicate effectively if you've never been taught how to handle difficult conversations. There are many reasons for ineffective communication, from cultural differences to lack of clarity to information overload.

This guide covers four common pitfalls:

1. Poor listening skills

2. Reacting quickly instead of responding intentionally

3. Criticizing and using "you" statements

4. Mind reading and making assumptions

CBT can significantly improve your communication by helping you identify and challenge unhelpful thinking patterns that can hinder communication, such as mind reading, personalizing, and jumping to conclusions. Through the use of various CBT tools and techniques, you can learn to enhance your perspective-taking ability, respond more mindfully, regulate your emotions, and effectively express your thoughts and feelings to others. Overall, this helps strengthen your relationships and make you a more confident and effective communicator.

Active Listening

You might notice that while someone else is speaking, you're already thinking about your response instead of truly hearing them. This can make the other person feel unheard or misunderstood, often causing conflicts. We all have a deep desire to be heard and understood. By honing your active listening skills, you can offer this to others, which in turn fosters deeper empathy and strengthens your relationships.

DIRECTIONS

1. During your next conversation, set an intention to be a better, more active listener.

2. While the other person is speaking, notice when your attention drifts. Be aware of moments when you're thinking about your response instead of listening.

3. Practice refocusing. When you catch your mind wandering, gently bring your focus back to the speaker. Aim to understand their perspective fully.

4. Summarize what you heard. After the person finishes speaking, try summarizing their main points. For example, "It sounds like you feel under-appreciated. You do so much at work and home, and you wish your efforts were acknowledged more."

5. Confirm your understanding. Don't assume you've understood correctly. Check with the speaker by asking, "Am I getting that right?"

Respond Thoughtfully

It's common to get caught up in emotions, especially in heated moments. Unfortunately, this can lead to saying things you later regret, potentially harming your relationships. If you struggle to express yourself calmly, learning to respond thoughtfully instead of reacting impulsively will be a big help. Unlike reacting, responding combines both logic and emotion, allowing for a more thoughtful and intentional approach that considers the consequences of what you say. It will take time and practice, but mastering this skill will help you engage in productive conversations and conduct yourself in a way that makes you feel proud.

DIRECTIONS

1. The next time you find yourself in a heated discussion, notice your impulse or urge to react immediately. Recognize the physical sensations shifting in your body. Feel yourself starting to get activated. Simply notice without judgment.

2. Resist the urge to act in this moment. Ground yourself by taking a few slow, deep breaths.

3. Pause with intention to consider the long-term impact of your response. How will this impact you, the other person, and your relationship?

4. If needed, take a time-out. Let the other person know that you need time to regulate. Commit to reconvening once you feel like you can engage in the conversation in a productive way. Use grounding techniques like the ones on page 89 to help you.

Use "I" Statements

When we're hurt by others, we often fall into criticizing or attacking mode. We point out what we believe others have done wrong instead of focusing on how their actions made us feel. Using "you" statements and pointing out someone else's wrongdoing immediately puts them on the defensive and can escalate conflict. It's much more productive to use "I" statements that focus on how you feel. This enables the other person to have more empathy for your position and promotes problem-solving. Here are a few examples:

SCENARIO	"YOU" STATEMENT	"I" STATEMENT
Your partner got home very late from work. You typically have dinner together each night. They didn't call to let you know they'd be late.	"You got home so late and didn't even think to call me. That's so inconsiderate of you. You couldn't even be bothered to pick up the phone."	"I became worried when it got late and I hadn't heard from you. I thought something was wrong. I would have appreciated it if you had reached out to me."
You are out to lunch with a friend who is focused on her phone. This has become a pattern of behavior whenever you hang out.	"You're always on the phone every time we hang out. It's like you don't even care what I have to say and are too distracted to even listen."	"I've noticed that you're on your phone more when we hang out. I feel disappointed when I see you on your phone, because it feels like what I'm saying isn't as important as what's happening on your phone."
You do a lot of work around the house. You feel like your partner doesn't notice and doesn't appreciate all you do.	"I do so much around the house. You completely take me for granted. You never even say thank you."	"I do a lot around the house. It takes a lot of time and effort. It hurts me to not feel appreciated or acknowledged."

1. Bring to mind a point of contention in one of your relationships. It could be something relatively minor or something major you'd like to address.

2. Identify how this makes you feel. Name the emotions this provokes for you. Do you feel sad, hurt, rejected, disappointed, etc.?

3. In your notebook or on a sheet of paper, practice writing an "I" statement that captures the way you feel.

4. When you next discuss this point of contention, use your "I" statement to express yourself.

5. Continue to practice using "I" statements in other situations to get more comfortable expressing yourself this way.

CBT TOOL

Combat Mind Reading

We often assume we know what others are thinking or intending without checking in with them. Mind reading not only causes us to spiral and overthink, but it can also lead to unnecessary conflict and miscommunication. To combat this cognitive distortion, seek evidence before jumping to conclusions; come from a place of curiosity and ask clarifying questions. For example, if a friend didn't reply to your text and you worry you've done something to upset them, you could be causing yourself unnecessary emotional turmoil with little confirmatory evidence. Instead of wasting precious mental energy, you can gain clarity by asking your friend if everything is okay.

DIRECTIONS

1. Notice when you are mind reading and making assumptions about other people's intentions.

2. Name it. Say, "I'm mind reading," or "I'm making assumptions."

3. Challenge your assumptions. If you believe "She must be upset with me," gather the evidence for and against that thought. Is there any evidence to suggest that's true? Is there any evidence to suggest that's untrue?

4. Depending on the nature of the situation, ask a clarifying question to allow the other person to share their perspective so that you can both move forward.

Additional CBT Tools

The following guides may also be helpful if you're struggling with communication:

* Anger (page 104)
* Fear (page 112)
* Guilt (page 118)
* People-Pleasing (page 159)
* Sadness (page 125)
* Shame (page 134)

In addition, these CBT skills may also be useful:

* Anger Iceberg (page 105)
* Body-Based Techniques for Anger (page 110)
* How to Respond to Anger Behaviorally (page 109)
* Identify Anger Triggers (page 107)
* Mindfulness of Emotions (page 129)
* Practice Assertive Communication (page 161)
* Thought Record (page 25)
* Validate Your Feelings (page 127)

Insomnia

The American Academy of Sleep Medicine reports that up to 33 percent of adults experience insomnia at least intermittently as well as 20 to 40 percent of children and teenagers. If you struggle with insomnia, you likely spend several hours trying to fall asleep and may struggle to stay asleep. This can lead to feelings of frustration and debilitating daytime fatigue. Sometimes insomnia exists on its own, but it is also quite common for insomnia to accompany other mental health challenges such as anxiety and depression.

Symptoms of insomnia include:

* Difficulty falling asleep
* Difficulty staying asleep—frequently waking up during the night or waking up early in the morning unable to fall back to sleep
* Sleep difficulties that cause distress in social life, career, education, or other important areas of functioning

Poor sleep hygiene habits can intensify insomnia symptoms. Other mental health challenges can also make insomnia worse in some people. For example, if you struggle with anxiety, depression, or even overthinking, this may make it more challenging to fall or stay asleep. What's more, clients I've worked with who have struggled with insomnia have been significantly impacted by their ability to get good-quality sleep, which often causes further anxiety and frustration that they feel toward sleeping.

CBT specifically designed to treat insomnia is called CBT-I. This approach helps you to track your sleep and understand how your daily routine impacts your sleep. CBT teaches you specific techniques such as bedtime restriction and encourages you to improve your sleep hygiene to support better-quality sleep. These following general sleep hygiene tips can be beneficial for anyone:

* Maintain a consistent bedtime and wake time.
* Take a walk and get sunlight exposure first thing in the morning. This helps to reset your circadian rhythm and signals to your brain to release melatonin, the sleep hormone, 12 to 14 hours after this initial light exposure.
* Avoid napping during the day.
* Limit caffeine intake. Avoid consuming any caffeine at least six hours prior to your bedtime.
* No screens one to two hours before bedtime. The blue light from your devices disrupts your circadian rhythm.
* Create a consistent evening routine. This helps signal to your brain that it's time to wind down and prepare for sleep.
* Carve out time to process your thoughts and feelings during the day. (This has been a game changer for some of my clients.) If you don't dedicate time to check in with yourself during the day, your mind will likely be occupied by certain thoughts the minute your head hits the pillow once the rest of the world is finally quiet.
* Practice mindfulness or meditation before bedtime.

Keep a Sleep Log

The first step in CBT treatment for insomnia is creating a sleep log. A sleep log provides a framework for you to track the details of your sleep over time and identify patterns. Here is a sample three-day sleep log:

	DAY 1	DAY 2	DAY 3
What time did I get into bed?			
What time did I try to fall asleep?			
How long did it take me to fall asleep (best estimate)?			
How many times did I wake up in the night?			
How long was my total time awake during the night (best estimate)?			
What time did I wake up for the day?			
What time did I get out of bed?			
How would I rate the quality of my sleep overall (very poor, poor, fair, good, very good)?			
Did I take any medication or use any substances that may have impacted my sleep?			
Overall notes: Was there any other noteworthy information about my sleep? Did I have bad dreams? Was I awake thinking about something specific?			

DIRECTIONS

1. Using the sample log as a go-by, create a sleep log for yourself, either electronically or on paper. Keep it in your bedroom in a handy spot.

2. Aim to complete your sleep log consistently for a minimum of two weeks.

3. Record your entries within one hour of waking up to ensure accuracy. Set an alarm or other notification to help remind you to fill it out.

4. Analyze your sleep data. What patterns do you notice? What areas of improvement can you identify? For example, is there a big gap of time between when you go to bed and when you actually try to fall asleep or between when you wake up and actually get out of bed?

5. Make any necessary adjustments and continue to log your sleep to keep making improvements over time.

Bedtime Restriction

There's a metric known as the sleep efficiency score, which can be used to measure how optimal your sleep is. Sleep efficiency is calculated by dividing your time asleep by your time spent in bed and multiplying that by 100 to get a percentage. For example, if you slept for six hours and spent eight hours total in bed, this would equal a sleep efficiency score of 75 percent.

In an ideal world, your time spent sleeping would more or less equal your time spent in bed. The concept of bedtime restriction in CBT helps you to optimize your overall sleep efficiency by limiting your time spent in bed beyond the time that you spend asleep.

GENERAL RULES

1. Determine your daily wake time based on your personal schedule. Determine your daily bedtime by subtracting your ideal number of hours of sleep from your wake time. Stick to this scheduled bedtime and wake time each day. Consistency is key. This will help you reset your circadian rhythm. (If you have a day in which you absolutely cannot stick to your bedtime because of life circumstances, still abide by your designated wake time to give yourself the greatest likelihood of maintaining your circadian rhythm.)

2. Do not nap during the day.

3. Do not do any activities in your bed other than sleeping and having sex. Use other areas of your home to read, scroll on your phone, watch TV, etc. You want your brain to associate your bed solely with sleep and no other activities.

4. Get into bed with the intention of going to sleep (not to begin another activity). Get out of bed as soon as your alarm goes off or you wake up for the day. Both of these behaviors help optimize your sleep efficiency score.

5. If you are having difficulty falling asleep and it's been longer than 20 minutes, get out of bed. Keep the lights dim and avoid looking at your phone or a

clock during this time. Resist calculating how much time you have until you must wake up in the morning. Do not do household chores or anything productive or goal oriented. Rather, do something boring. Wait until your body gives you clear clues that you're getting sleepy to get back into bed and try falling asleep again.

Note: *My clients often resist this technique. They think, "Why am I getting out of bed if I'm trying to sleep?" On the surface, it may seem counterintuitive. However, it's actually a powerful principle because it keeps your brain from associating your bed with anything other than sleep.*

Challenge Your Sleep-Related Beliefs

If you struggle with insomnia, it's likely you have beliefs about sleep that add to your feelings of frustration and anxiety toward your relationship with sleep. When you challenge those beliefs and arrive at more helpful ones, you will likely notice a decrease in frustration and anxiety. Challenging these untrue and unhelpful beliefs about sleep will help you in the moments when you spiral about what your lack of sleep might mean or what it might contribute to.

DIRECTIONS

1. Take inventory of the beliefs that you have about sleep that contribute to feelings of anxiety or frustration that you feel about your relationship to sleep. Some examples are:

   * "I need at least eight hours of sleep to be able to function."

   * "If I don't sleep enough, I need to nap the next day or sleep longer to catch up on sleep."

   * "I might totally lose control over my ability to sleep."

   * "If I sleep poorly for one night, the rest of my week will be thrown off."

2. Conduct a behavior experiment to test these beliefs. For example, if you believe you won't be able to function the next day after minimal sleep, test that prediction: After a poor night of sleep, gather evidence the following day to either prove or disprove your prediction. Is it true that you were unable to function, or did you successfully make it through your day? Chances are, you made it through the day.

3. Come up with a more helpful belief based on your experiment. For example, "Even if I don't get a full night's sleep, I can still function during the day."

Additional CBT Tools

The following guides may also be helpful if you're struggling with insomnia:

* Anxiety (page 22)
* Chronic Stress (page 43)
* Depression (page 51)
* Inner Critic (page 62)
* Overthinking (page 84)

In addition, these CBT skills may also be useful:

* Behavioral Activation (page 55)
* Best, Worst, Most Realistic Outcome (page 90)
* Change How You Think About Stress (page 46)
* Designated Worry Time (page 87)
* Grounding Techniques (page 89)
* Mindfulness of Thoughts Meditation (page 91)
* Practice Mindfulness and Body-Based Techniques (page 48)
* Thought Defusion Techniques (page 85)
* Thought Record (page 25)
* Wheel of Life (page 53)

People-Pleasing

People-pleasing is related to the "fawn" response. Rather than fighting, feeling, or freezing in stressful situations, people-pleasers respond to threats by "fawning" or engaging in behavior that's meant to appease others. In the long run, people-pleasing can leave you feeling depleted and resentful and negatively impact your relationships. People-pleasing behaviors tend to stem from a desire for acceptance, fear of rejection, or low self-esteem.

Signs of people-pleasing include:

* Sacrificing your own needs for the sake of others
* Struggling to voice your feelings
* Fearing others will be disappointed in you
* Avoiding conflict at all costs
* Feeling resentful in your relationships
* Mirroring other people's opinions and not sharing yours
* Overapologizing when it's not necessary
* Having difficulty saying no or setting boundaries
* Being overly passive when communicating

If you're struggling with people-pleasing, you might:

THINK	FEEL	ACT
"I can't speak up." "I'm worried that they're upset with me." "I want everybody to like me and be pleased with me." "I have to gain others' approval." "I can't handle conflict." "I shouldn't do anything to challenge the status quo."	Depleted from doing so much for others Taken for granted or taken advantage of Resentful in your relationships Low self-confidence Afraid of conflict Worried others are upset with you Unfulfilled by your relationships	Overapologize Say yes when you want to say no Help others even if it's inconvenient for you Communicate passively Defer to other people's opinions Avoid conflict Ignore your needs and desires Stay quiet

People-pleasing typically originates in early childhood. It's a way of appeasing others to keep yourself safe. In extreme cases, if you grew up in a household where there was neglect, trauma, or abuse, you may have learned to people-please to keep yourself safe and avoid conflict. As a child, people-pleasing may have helped you avoid abandonment and protect yourself from harm. However, as an adult, continuing to engage in people-pleasing behaviors may actually lead to resentment in relationships, not getting your needs met, and feeling like you're being taken for granted.

Understanding the origins of your people-pleasing behavior and showing compassion to the part of you that was doing its best to cope will eventually allow you to relearn new ways of coping that will serve you better moving forward. CBT can help you identify the patterns, beliefs, and behaviors that keep you stuck in the cycle of people-pleasing. It then guides you in becoming more assertive, setting boundaries, and advocating for your needs, creating healthier and more balanced relationships where your needs are respected.

Practice Assertive Communication

Communication exists on a spectrum from overly passive to overly aggressive, as shown in figure 5.1. Passive communication is prioritizing the needs, wants, and feelings of others at your own expense, and aggressive communication is expressing that only your needs, wants, and feelings matter. In most cases, the goal is to aim for assertive communication, which strikes the perfect balance by emphasizing the importance of both your needs and others' needs.

If you tend to be passive, you might worry that you're coming across as aggressive when you're trying to be assertive. In my experience, clients who express this concern are rarely being aggressive. Instead, they just need more practice with assertiveness.

PASSIVE
My needs don't matter.

ASSERTIVE
All of our needs matter.

AGGRESSIVE
Only my needs matter.

Figure 5.1: The Communication Spectrum

DIRECTIONS

1. Grab a pen and paper or your notebook. Bring to mind a recent situation in which you were asked to do something. You didn't have the bandwidth to do it, but you agreed anyway. Describe the situation. Here's an example:

   Situation: Your friend who is a new mom asks you to pick up something at the grocery store, but you don't have the time to do it today.

2. Write out the passive, aggressive, and assertive responses to this request. Here's an example of each:

> **Passive response:** "Sure, I guess I can do that. Do you need anything else?"

> **Aggressive response:** "Absolutely not. I have such a busy day! Don't you know how busy I am?"

> **Assertive response:** "I'm not able to make it to the store today since my schedule is full. I may have time later this week if you're not able to make it by then."

3. Practice saying each response aloud. Notice how you feel as you do so. When saying the assertive response, use a confident tone, keep your eyes up, and your shoulders back. Remember, your needs, wants, and desires are just as valid as those of others.

4. As you practice assertive communication with others, keep the following tips in mind:

    * Use "I" statements to express how you feel.
    * Clearly express your boundary, need, or expectation.
    * Use a confident tone of voice and keep your head held high.
    * Be conscious of the tendency to overapologize.
    * Remember that your needs are valid.
    * Normalize that it's going to feel uncomfortable at first.
    * Self-soothe that part of you that fears rejection for speaking up.

5. Keep practicing until it begins to feel more comfortable.

Note: *If you're hesitant to practice assertiveness because you fear it may lead to negative outcomes in your relationships, explore your underlying beliefs about assertive communication. You might think, "If I speak up, it will lead to conflict," or "It's not safe for me to voice my needs," or "If I disappoint someone, it means I'm a bad person." If you identify with any of these beliefs, refer to the Challenge Rules and Assumptions tool on page 97.*

Challenge People-Pleasing Behaviors

Making small behavior changes can help you build confidence in speaking up for yourself and voicing your needs. Each time you challenge old people-pleasing tendencies, you gradually increase your self-assurance.

DIRECTIONS

1. Do a behavioral experiment by identifying a people-pleasing behavior you want to change and what specifically you plan to practice. Here are some ideas:

   * Instead of always deferring to your friend's choice, suggest a meeting place.

   * If your order is wrong, ask the barista to remake your coffee.

   * Instead of pretending you don't care or that you agree, share your opinion honestly.

   * Rather than stay late, leave work on time.

   * Instead of letting something slide, let your partner know how their behavior affects you.

   * When you don't want to accept an invitation, say no.

   * Set a boundary that respects your time, energy, and needs.

   * When something makes you uncomfortable, speak up.

2. Note your predictions: What do you think will happen if you do this experiment?

3. Decide when and where you will practice this behavior during the week.

4. At the appointed time and place, execute your experiment.

5. Reflect: Did your predictions come true? Was the outcome different than you imagined? What did you learn? How can you continue to practice this new behavior?

Coping Statements

Coping statements are a powerful tool to help ground you during moments of distress. Reminding yourself of these truths can ease the discomfort that comes from setting boundaries or voicing your needs and opinions. If you struggle with people-pleasing, you might question whether it's safe to speak up, fear conflict, and prioritize others over yourself. Coping statements remind you that it is safe to voice your needs and take care of yourself first.

DIRECTIONS

1. Write out a coping statement that resonates with you and put it in a place you can easily access such as on your phone or a sticky note on your mirror. Here are some of my favorite coping statements for people-pleasing behaviors to get you started:

    * I don't need to explain myself. I can simply say no.

    * It's not my responsibility to take care of others' emotions around me.

    * Conflict is a normal part of any relationship.

    * I am an adult now, and it is safe to speak up and voice my needs in relationships.

    * Feeling guilty after setting a boundary doesn't mean that I did something wrong.*

    * I am learning to be assertive and stand up for my inner child, who felt unsafe speaking up.

    * I am not for everyone, and I am okay with that.

2. Notice how the statement makes you feel both emotionally and physically when you read it.

3. Refer to this coping statement as often as you need to.

* If guilt arises after setting a boundary or saying no, remember that this is a normal part of the process. The guilt doesn't mean you've done something wrong; it indicates you're engaging in a new behavior that will take time to get used to. If these feelings persist, you may find it helpful to read the "Guilt" guide on page 118.

Additional CBT Tools

The following guides may also be helpful if you're struggling with people-pleasing:

* Anxiety (page 22)
* Chronic Stress (page 43)
* Guilt (page 118)
* Ineffective Communication (page 144)
* Inner Critic (page 62)
* Perfectionism (page 93)
* Procrastination (page 166)

In addition, these CBT skills may also be useful:

* Behavioral Experiment (page 99)
* Challenge Rules and Assumptions (page 97)
* Mindfulness of Emotions (page 129)
* Thought Record (page 25)
* Use "I" Statements (page 147)

Procrastination

Procrastination is a form of avoidance that involves delaying or putting off tasks, often leading to increased stress, anxiety, and potential negative consequences. It is frequently misunderstood and wrongly associated with laziness or a lack of caring. My clients often say, "I can't get started. It makes me feel so lazy," or "Maybe if I cared more about this, I'd have an easier time doing it." In reality, procrastination is a complex behavior with various underlying causes.

I often see procrastination used as a coping mechanism to avoid emotional discomfort. Projects or tasks can trigger feelings of overwhelm, anxiety, perfectionism, frustration, or boredom, which can feel too intense to cope with. It's often easier to put off tasks or avoid them altogether than to confront those feelings head-on.

Here are a few common emotional and psychological causes of procrastination:

* Overwhelm: feeling so overwhelmed by a project that it seems daunting and not knowing where to start
* Anxiety: worrying about the outcome of a task
* Perfectionism: setting unrealistic standards of perfection for a task and fearing that it won't be perfect
* Boredom: feeling apathetic, disengaged, or lacking interest in a task
* Fear of failure: fearing not meeting expectations or failing at a task

CBT helps with procrastination by helping you understand the root cause of why you procrastinate. By uncovering your automatic thoughts triggered by a particular task and the subsequent feelings, you can begin to understand the underlying cause of your procrastination and how to overcome avoidance. CBT also provides practical tips and techniques that enable you to initiate tasks and overcome avoidance.

Predict Time and Difficulty

Have you ever dreaded a task, building it up in your mind, only to find it wasn't nearly as bad as you thought? This happens to me often with things like making phone calls or going to the post office. One major trigger for procrastination is the anticipation of pain and difficulty. So often we overestimate how painful or boring a task will be as well as how long it will take, thus making the task seem incredibly daunting.

Practicing more accurate predictions can help reduce the anxiety or avoidance associated with tasks over time. This shift in perspective helps you realize, "This task won't be as bad as I'm imagining. I've tackled challenging tasks in the past, so I know I can do this." This will increase your confidence in your ability to manage challenging tasks in the future.

DIRECTIONS

1. Grab a pen and paper or your notebook, and create a log sheet that looks like this:

Describe the Task:			
BEFORE THE TASK	**PREDICTION**	**AFTER THE TASK**	**ACTUAL OUTCOME**
How much time do you predict the task will take?		How much time did the task actually take?	
How painful do you believe the task will be?		How painful did the task actually feel?	

2. Before you do a task that you've been putting off, describe what it is and fill in your predictions.

3. Do the task, and once it's complete, fill in the actual outcome.

4. Use this log sheet for a week to gather consistent data. Fill it out each time you tackle a challenging task or something you've been putting off.

5. At the end of the week, reflect on your takeaways from this exercise. Ask yourself:

   * How did the length of time I predicted compare to how long the task took in reality?

   * How did the level of pain I predicted compare to how painful it felt in reality?

   * Are there any patterns in the data?

   * What takeaways can I gather from the patterns I see?

   * What will I remind myself the next time I sense myself avoiding a specific task?

Set Realistic Expectations

The connection between perfectionism and procrastination often gets overlooked. Contrary to the misconception that procrastination stems from laziness or indifference, it's often driven by the desire for perfection. When you care deeply about the outcome, the fear of not meeting high standards can make a task feel intimidating or unapproachable.

DIRECTIONS

1. Grab a pen and paper or your notebook. Write down any beliefs you have about the task or the standards you feel you must meet. For example:

    *   "This needs to be perfect."

    *   "I can't make any mistakes."

    *   "This has to be the most impressive thing I've ever written."

2. Notice how these beliefs make you feel and the resistance that they create.

3. Challenge these unhelpful beliefs. Ask yourself:

    *   Is it reasonable to expect perfection right away?

    *   Would I hold others to this same standard?

    *   Is it possible to make edits and improvements later on in the process?

    *   Would I rather have something be done imperfectly or not at all?

4. Set realistic expectations for yourself. Write out those expectations. For example:

    *   "This is my first draft. I can get my ideas down on paper and worry about the quality later."

    *   "Making mistakes is a part of the process."

    *   "I wouldn't hold someone else to the standard of perfection right away, so I don't need to hold myself to that unrealistic standard, either."

5. Notice how these new beliefs make you feel. Remind yourself often of your new beliefs to reinforce them throughout the process.

6. Unburden yourself from the need for it to be perfect and take action. In addition to the Pomodoro Timer, which is up next, the Five-Minute Rule on page 36 can help you get started.

CBT TOOL

Pomodoro Timer

The Pomodoro Timer is a tool that helps you work in focused intervals, structuring your tasks and planning specific break times to increase productivity. Setting a timer for a limited time can create just enough of a sense of urgency to get started on a task. It also helps gamify a task if you approach the work time with the mindset of seeing how much you can accomplish within that time frame. Finally, it also helps your brain to know that a break is coming. You don't need to be tethered to your desk indefinitely. The traditional Pomodoro Timer involves 25 minutes of work followed by a 5-minute break, but you can modify it to 45 minutes of work followed by a 15-minute break if you prefer.

DIRECTIONS

1. Access the online Pomodoro Timer at PomoFocus.io. You can also use any timer you have available.

2. Decide on a task you need to accomplish. It could be anything from folding laundry or tidying up the kitchen to sending out holiday cards or replying to emails. Get as specific as possible.

3. Start a timer for 25 minutes. Begin working on the task.

4. Once the 25 minutes is up, set a timer for 5 minutes. Take a 5-minute break. To make the most of your break, avoid activities like scrolling on your phone or going online. Instead, drink water, have a snack, stretch, use the restroom, or take a short walk.

5. Repeat this cycle as many times as you need to until the task at hand is complete.

Additional CBT Tools

The following guides may also be helpful if you're struggling with procrastination:

* ADHD (page 34)
* Depression (page 51)
* Lack of Motivation (page 69)
* Perfectionism (page 93)
* Unhealthy Habits (page 173)

If difficulty regulating emotions leads you to procrastinate, the following guides may also be helpful:

* Anger (page 104)
* Fear (page 112)
* Guilt (page 118)
* Sadness (page 125)
* Shame (page 134)

In addition, these CBT skills may also be useful:

* Avoid All-or-Nothing Thinking (page 175)
* Cultivate Your "Why" (page 73)
* Eisenhower Matrix (page 37)
* Five-Minute Rule (page 36)
* Gamify Your Tasks (page 40)
* Graded Tasks (page 71)
* Identify Triggers and Cope Ahead (page 176)
* Improve Your Self-Talk (page 75)
* Limit Distractions (page 39)
* Mindfulness of Emotions (page 129)
* Set Timers (page 41)
* Start Small with Manageable Goals (page 177)
* Thought Record (page 25)
* Validate Your Feelings (page 127)
* Visualize How You'll Feel Afterward (page 74)

Unhealthy Habits

Habits are behaviors or actions repeated so regularly that they often become automatic, requiring little conscious thought. These habits can be either beneficial or detrimental, depending on their short-term and long-term effects. There are several reasons we stick to unhealthy habits despite knowing their negative impact. Habits form through repetition; the more we repeat an action, the more automatic it becomes. This process ingrains the habit in our brains, making many of our unhealthy behaviors occur without conscious awareness. Understanding these mental processes shows that breaking ingrained habits and developing new ones requires time, effort, consistency, and repetition.

Unhealthy habits are also tempting to engage in because of our brain's reward system and the release of dopamine we experience in response to pleasurable activities. This feel-good chemical keeps us coming back for more despite the potentially damaging long-term impact of some of these unhealthy habits. Moreover, since many of these consequences are not immediate, this can also make it challenging to ditch unhealthy habits. We may understand consciously that our unhealthy habit has a negative long-term consequence, but that often doesn't outweigh the feel-good hit we experience in the moment.

I believe much of this is caused by an inability to tolerate uncomfortable emotions. We're driven to social media, smoking, junk food, or worse to distract, numb, and/or lessen the intensity of the discomfort. That's why developing emotion regulation skills is critical in the process of letting go of unhealthy habits. Over time, we learn we are capable of coping with uncomfortable emotions without using unhealthy habits to cope.

That said, cultivating new, healthier habits is challenging. Habit formation takes time and consistent effort. People often get discouraged and quit before giving themselves enough time to establish a new habit. Unlike unhealthy habits that provide an immediate dopamine reward, healthier habits like eating well and exercising often take longer to show results. This requires patience, which can be difficult because our brains are wired to seek short-term rewards. Additionally, a lack of support, accountability, or a clearly defined plan can make it easy to lose motivation and direction. Understanding these challenges can help us approach the process with more compassion and perseverance, ultimately leading to lasting positive change.

CBT can be a powerful tool for breaking old habits and establishing new ones. CBT helps you identify the triggers that lead to unhealthy habits and develop emotion regulation skills, so you don't have to rely on those habits to self-soothe. In creating new habits, CBT assists you in setting clearly defined goals and encourages you to think and speak to yourself in ways that support those goals. This approach not only fosters positive change but also empowers you to maintain it.

Avoid All-or-Nothing Thinking

When we think in black-or-white or all-or-nothing terms, it's hard to view progress as nonlinear and incremental. We might see one slipup as a failure and give up, instead of recognizing that minor setbacks are part of the process. A slipup doesn't erase all the effort we've put in so far.

Let's look at some examples:

* **OLD THOUGHT:** "I'll never be able to stick with meditating every day."

   REFRAMED THOUGHT: "I know forming new habits takes time. I'll try my best to show up each day. If I miss a day, I can start again tomorrow."

* **OLD THOUGHT:** "I already had one drink, so I might as well have a few more."

   REFRAMED THOUGHT: "I can choose to make a different choice at any moment. It doesn't have to be all-or-nothing."

* **OLD THOUGHT:** "I slipped up, so I totally blew it."

   REFRAMED THOUGHT: "One slip-up doesn't mean I blew it. It doesn't erase all the progress I've made so far."

Do you see how the old thoughts inhibit growth, while the reframed thoughts support sustainable behavior changes in the long term?

DIRECTIONS

1. When you're about to engage in an unhealthy habit or struggle to build a new healthy one, notice what you tell yourself. What is your automatic thought?

2. Challenge the automatic thought. Is that thought entirely true? Is it helpful?

3. Reframe the thought. What thought would be more helpful and supportive in this moment? What's a more balanced perspective?

4. Keep reinforcing the more positive, supportive thought.

5. Consistently practice these steps to shift your mindset to better support your goals and foster lasting change.

Identify Triggers and Cope Ahead

Habits are always tied to specific triggers, which can be thoughts, emotions, situations, or environments. By identifying your triggers, you can plan ahead and create strategies for how to approach them when they arise in the future.

DIRECTIONS

1. For the next week, keep track of what triggers you to engage in a habit you want to break.

2. Each time you feel the urge, note the following: (1) Where were you? (2) What were you doing? (3) How were you feeling? and (4) What were you thinking? For example, let's say you want to break the habit of vaping. Throughout the week, you might notice:

    *   Thoughts: "I'll just have one puff" and "I need it to be able to focus."
    *   Emotions: stress, boredom
    *   Situations: studying for exams, out with friends at a party
    *   Environments: my bedroom, friend's house

3. Cope ahead. Develop a plan of action for each trigger you identify. Be specific and think about how to approach each trigger mindfully.

    *   Thoughts: What will you tell yourself when these tempting thoughts arise?
    *   Emotions: How can you cope more effectively with stress and boredom?
    *   Situations: How will you approach studying or being out at parties differently? How can you be around others who may be engaging in the habit you're looking to break?
    *   Environments: What can you do to make your environment more conducive to your goals?

4. Practice your new responses. The next time you face the triggers you tracked, actively use the coping strategies you developed.

Start Small with Manageable Goals

Setting yourself up for success is crucial when cultivating new habits. Approachable and achievable goals help build positive momentum, leading to sustainable behavior change over time. The SMART goal framework—specific, measurable, achievable, relevant, and time-bound—can be particularly effective in this process. SMART goals are actionable and give you a clear, tangible thing to strive toward.

Here are some examples of SMART goals and goals that aren't so smart to help you see the differences:

NEW HABIT	NON-SMART GOAL	SMART GOAL
Running	"I want to run more."	"I will commit to going on a 10-minute run four times this week before work. I will work my way up to 30 minutes by the end of the next three months. I will track my weekly progress using a running app."
Reducing Phone Use	"I want to stop scrolling on my phone so much."	"I will put my phone in the other room 30 minutes before bed to limit my nighttime scrolling. I will set a nightly reminder at 8 p.m. each night and track my screen time using a tracking app."

NEW HABIT	NON-SMART GOAL	SMART GOAL
Meditating	"I want to meditate."	"I will meditate daily for five minutes in the evening after I put my kids to bed. I will keep track of my meditation sessions in my notebook, which I already write in before bed."

DIRECTIONS

1. Identify a goal. What habit are you looking to break or build into your regular routine?

2. Outline that goal using the SMART framework.

   * Specific: What exactly do you want to accomplish?

   * Measurable: How will you measure your progress?

   * Achievable: Is this a realistic goal considering your current situation and resources?

   * Relevant: Why is this goal important to you? How does it align with your values?

   * Time-bound: What is your target completion date? Are there smaller milestones along the way?

3. Keep track of your progress in a way that works for you. Celebrate your wins along the way and give yourself credit where credit is due.

Habit-Related Bonus Strategies

There are many useful strategies for building new habits and breaking old ones. Experiment with each of these tools to see which work best for you. You may find that a combination of strategies is just what you need:

* **Create barriers for unhealthy habits:** Make it more challenging to engage in unhealthy habits to ensure that doing so becomes an intentional choice rather than an automatic action.
* **Practice habit stacking:** Pair the new habit you want to build with an existing habit that you already do consistently to integrate the new habit into your routine more seamlessly.
* **Utilize accountability:** Share your goals with someone to provide additional motivation and support.
* **Set reminders:** Create daily reminders to reinforce new habits until they become automatic.

DIRECTIONS

1. Identify an unhealthy habit you want to break. What barriers can you create to make engaging in these habits more difficult? Here are some examples:

    * Reduce soda consumption: Don't keep soda in your home. Each time you're tempted to have soda, you'll have to make the effort to go out and buy it, adding a layer of intentionality.

    * Limit YouTube time: Remove the YouTube app or shortcut from your device. Instead of clicking it automatically, you'll need to consciously download the app or type in the URL when you want to use it, making you more aware of your actions.

2. Identify a new habit you want to build. What existing habit can you stack it with to make it easier to remember and do consistently? For example:

* Take supplements: If you want to commit to taking your daily supplements, do it right after brushing your teeth each morning.

3. Identify a new habit you want to build. Who can you recruit to help you stay accountable? How can they support you in achieving your goals? For example:

   * Go for regular walks: If you want to go on walks more regularly, recruit a friend to be your walking buddy. This makes the activity more enjoyable and adds a layer of commitment.

4. Identify a new habit you want to build. Set daily reminders to help you remember to enforce and practice this habit until it becomes automatic. For example:

   * Drink more water: Set alarms throughout the day to remind you to hydrate. Over time, this will help make drinking water a more regular part of your routine.

Additional CBT Tools

The following guides may also be helpful if you're struggling with unhealthy habits:

* ADHD (page 34)
* Depression (page 51)
* Lack of Motivation (page 69)
* Procrastination (page 166)

If difficulty regulating emotions leads you to engage in unhealthy habits, the following guides may also be helpful:

* Anger (page 104)
* Fear (page 112)
* Guilt (page 118)
* Sadness (page 125)
* Shame (page 134)

In addition, these CBT skills may also be useful:

* Cultivate Your "Why" (page 73)
* Five-Minute Rule (page 36)
* Graded Tasks (page 71)
* Improve Your Self-Talk (page 75)
* Limit Distractions (page 39)
* Mindfulness of Emotions (page 129)
* Pomodoro Timer (page 171)
* Practice Self-Compassion (page 67)
* Predict Time and Difficulty (page 167)
* Set Realistic Expectations (page 169)
* Set Timers (page 41)
* Thought Record (page 25)
* Validate Your Feelings (page 127)
* Visualize How You'll Feel Afterward (page 74)

RESOURCES

Books

The Anxiety and Worry Workbook: The Cognitive Behavioral Solution
by David A. Clark, PhD, and Aaron T. Beck, MD

Atlas of the Heart: Mapping Meaningful Connection and the Language of Human Experience by Brené Brown, PhD, MSW

Feeling Good: The New Mood Therapy by David D. Burns, MD

The Feeling Good Handbook by David D. Burns, MD

Mind Over Mood: Change How You Feel by Changing the Way You Think
by Dennis Greenberger, PhD, and Christine A. Padesky, PhD

Self-Compassion: The Proven Power of Being Kind to Yourself
by Kristin Neff, PhD

CBT-Related Apps

Clarity: CBT Self-Help Journal: www.thinkwithclarity.com/

MindShift CBT Anxiety Relief: www.anxietycanada.com/resources/mindshift-cbt/

MoodTools Depression Aid: moodtools.org

CBT Therapist Directories

Association for Behavioral and Cognitive Therapies (ACBT) Services: services.abct
.org/i4a/memberDirectory/index.cfm?directory_id=3&pageID=3282

Beck Institute CBT Certified Clinician Directory: cares.beckinstitute.org/get
-treatment/clinician-directory/

Emotion Vocabulary/Self-Compassion

The Ekmans' Atlas of Emotions: atlasofemotions.org

Kristin Neff's work and research: self-compassion.org

Mindfulness and Meditation

Calm app: calm.com

Headspace app: headspace.com

Insight Timer app: insighttimer.com

Ten Percent Happier app: meditatehappier.com/explore-happier-meditation

Sharon Salzberg's meditations and work: SharonSalzberg.com

Tara Brach's meditations and offerings: TaraBrach.com

REFERENCES

American Academy of Sleep Medicine. "Provider Fact Sheet: Insomnia." AASM.org. July 2022. Accessed March 3, 2025. https://aasm.org/wp-content /uploads/2022/07/ProviderFS-Insomnia.pdf.

American Psychiatric Association. "What Is ADHD?" Psychiatry.org. Last reviewed June 2022. https://www.psychiatry.org/patients-families/adhd/what-is-adhd.

Bandura, Albert. *Social Foundations of Thought and Action: A Social Cognitive Theory.* Prentice Hall, 1985.

Beck, Aaron T. *Cognitive Therapy and the Emotional Disorders*. Penguin Books, 1976.

Beck, Aaron T., A. John Rush, Brian F. Shaw, Gary Emery, Robert J. DeRubeis, and Steven D. Hollon. *Cognitive Therapy of Depression*. Guilford Press, 1979.

Beck, Judith S. *Cognitive Behavior Therapy: Basics and Beyond.* 2nd ed. Guilford Press, 2011.

Brown, Brené. *Atlas of the Heart: Mapping Meaningful Connection and the Language of Human Experience.* Random House, 2021.

Brown, Brené. "Shame Resilience Theory: A Grounded Theory Study on Women and Shame." *Families in Society* 87, no. 1 (2006): 43–52. https://doi .org/10.1606/1044-3894.3483.

Clear, James. *Atomic Habits: An Easy & Proven Way to Build Good Habits & Break Bad Ones.* Avery, 2018.

Greenberger, Dennis, and Christine A. Padesky. *Mind Over Mood: Change How You Feel by Changing the Way You Think.* 2nd ed. Guilford Press, 2015.

Huberman, Andrew, host. *Huberman Lab Podcast.* "ADHD & How Anyone Can Improve Their Focus." Huberman Lab, September 12, 2021. https://www .hubermanlab.com/episode/adhd-and-how-anyone-can-improve-their-focus.

Linehan, Marsha M. *DBT Skills Training Manual.* 2nd ed. Guilford Press, 2014.

National Center for Health Statistics. "Attention Deficit Hyperactivity Disorder (ADHD)." US Centers for Disease Control and Prevention. Accessed February 26, 2025. https://www.cdc.gov/nchs/fastats/adhd.htm.

Nezu, Christine Maguth, and Arthur M. Nezu, eds. *The Oxford Handbook of Cognitive and Behavioral Therapies*. Oxford University Press, 2015.

Nikolić, Milica, Laurie J. Hannigan, Georgina Krebs, Abram Sterne, Alice M. Gregory, and Thalia C. Eley. "Aetiology of Shame and Its Association with Adolescent Depression and Anxiety: Results from a Prospective Twin and Sibling Study." *The Journal of Child Psychology and Psychiatry* 63, no. 1 (2022): 99–108. https://doi.org/10.1111/jcpp.13465.

Rotter, Julian B. *Social Learning and Clinical Psychology*. Prentice Hall, 1954.

INDEX

Hayes, Steven, 10
hopelessness, 51, 52, 78
"hot" thoughts, 13

I

"if-then" statements, 97
imperfection, 93, 94, 95, 98, 99, 169
impulse control, 34, 146
inner critic, 62–63, 68, 93
    Challenge Your "Faulty" Beliefs About Self-Criticism, 65–66
    Get to Know Your Inner Critic, 64
    Practice Self-Compassion, 67
    See also self-criticism
insecurity, 105
insomnia, 14, 151–52, 158
    Bedtime Restriction, 155–56
    Challenge Your Sleep-Related Beliefs, 157
    Keep a Sleep Log, 153–54
interpersonal effectiveness, 10
isolation, social, 51, 52, 55, 131, 134, 140
"I" Statements, Use, 147–48

J

judgment, 17, 91, 127, 134, 140, 146
    of emotions, 129
    fear of, 31, 112, 140
    non-, 15, 19, 27, 48, 49, 67

K

kindness, 14, 56, 65, 80

L

labels, unfair, 17
laziness, 65, 75, 166, 169
lethargy, 51, 52
Linehan, Marsha, 10
listening skills, 144, 145

loneliness, 52, 105
love, 94, 96, 134

M

meditation, 19, 48, 91, 152
Meyer, Paul J., 53
mindfulness, 10, 15, 19, 45, 152
    of emotions, 125, 126, 129–30
    Mindfulness of Emotions, 129–30
    Mindfulness of Thoughts Meditation, 91
    Practice Mindfulness and Body-Based Techniques, 48–49
mind reading, 17, 144, 149
motivation, 14, 34, 36, 69–70, 76, 174
    Cultivate Your "Why," 73
    Graded Tasks, 71–72
    Improve Your Self-Talk, 75
    Visualize How You'll Feel Afterward, 74

N

naming emotions, 14, 49, 106, 127, 130, 148
nervousness, 22, 105
nervous system, 15, 48–49, 89, 109

O

overthinking, 15, 84, 92, 151
    Best, Worst, Most Realistic Outcome, 90
    Designated Worry Time, 87–88
    Grounding Techniques, 89
    Mindfulness of Thoughts Meditation, 91
    Thought Defusion Techniques, 15, 85–86

overwhelm, 14, 35, 37, 44, 105, 166
    graded tasks help with, 71–72

P

panic, 22, 24
Participation Pie, 121–22
passivity, 159–60, 161–62
people-pleasing, 119, 159–60, 165
    Challenge People-Pleasing Behaviors, 163
    Coping Statements, 164
    Practice Assertive Communication, 161–62
perfectionism, 62, 63, 93–95, 100
    Behavioral Experiment, 99
    Bring Awareness to Your Perfectionism, 96
    Challenge Rules and Assumptions, 97–98
    procrastination and, 166, 169
personalization, 18, 108, 116, 144
phobias, 12, 22, 24
physiological responses, 9, 31, 44–45, 49, 110
Pomodoro Timer, 171
popular psychology, 62, 63
positive reinforcement, 40
problem-solving skills, 25, 46, 90, 147
procrastination, 14, 34, 93, 94, 166, 172
    Predict Time and Difficulty, 167–68
    Set Realistic Expectations, 169–70
productivity, 65, 87, 146, 147, 156, 171
proprioceptive grounding, 89

R

reassurance-seeking, 23–24, 113
regret, 105, 118, 120, 146

ACKNOWLEDGMENTS

To my mentors, teachers, and colleagues, thank you for guiding and inspiring me. I have learned so much from your collaboration.

To Clara Song Lee, my editor, thank you for trusting me with this project. It's been such a joy to work with you to bring this book to life. I'm honored to share it with the world.

To my past, present, and future clients, thank you for your openness and courage. Most of all, thank you for trusting me to be a part of your mental health journey.

To my parents, thank you for everything. I am eternally grateful.

To Tyler, thank you for being my rock.

ABOUT THE AUTHOR

Gianna LaLota, LMHC, LPC, is a New York–based therapist, speaker, and the founder of Mindful Mental Health Counseling, a practice that serves clients based in New York and New Jersey. Gianna works with adults struggling with anxiety and incorporates elements of mindfulness into her work with clients. Gianna specializes in cognitive behavioral therapy (CBT) and dialectical behavior therapy (DBT). She is a licensed yoga teacher (RYT 500) and is certified in Reiki and EFT tapping. Gianna has a growing online community on Instagram, where she shares about mindful mental health @mindfultherapynyc. Learn more at NYCMindfulMentalHealthCounseling.com.

Hi there,

We hope *Think, Act, and Feel Better with CBT* helped you. If you have any questions or concerns about your book, or have received a damaged copy, please contact customerservice@penguinrandomhouse.com. We're here and happy to help.

Also, please consider writing a review on your favorite retailer's website to let others know what you thought of the book.

Sincerely,

The Zeitgeist Team